COLLINS
COBUILD

KEY WORDS IN BUSINESS

Bill Mascull

HarperCollins*Publishers*

HarperCollins Publishers
77-85 Fulham Palace Road
London W6 8JB

COBUILD is a trademark of William Collins Sons & Co Ltd

First published 1996
Reprinted 1997 (twice), 1998, 1999

6 8 10 9 7 5

ISBN 0 00 375045 0

Design and typesetting by
eMC Design, Bromham, Bedfordshire

Printed and bound in Great Britain by
Caledonian International Book Manufacturing Ltd.

We would also like to thank Elaine Allen and Adrian Pilbeam for their helpful comments on the text.

Corpus Acknowledgements

We would like to acknowledge the assistance of the many hundreds of individuals and companies who have kindly given permission for copyright material to be used in The Bank of English. The written sources include many national and regional newspapers in Britain and overseas; magazine and periodical publishers; and book publishers in Britain, the United States, and Australia. Extensive spoken data has been provided by radio and television broadcasting companies; research workers at many universities and other institutions; and numerous individual contributors. We are grateful to them all.

www.cobuild.collins.co.uk

Contents

Introduction

Key Words in Business is designed to help you understand and use essential business vocabulary in English.

It systematically covers words and expressions that frequently occur and recur in talking about business. Some of these occur almost exclusively in business contexts; others are used in general English but are used in a particular way when talking about business.

This book shows what these words and expressions mean, how they are used and how they relate to each other.

Key Words in Business covers six main subject areas. You look at the meanings of frequently occurring words in these areas in the context of real examples from newspapers and business books.

You then go on to apply and develop your knowledge of meaning and usage in specially devised language activities, many of them based on longer extracts and articles. These have been chosen for their topicality, and for their relevance to everyone interested in business.

Key Words in Business has been written so that each chapter can be read sequentially from beginning to end. Or you may just want to dip and browse, looking at things that interest you. A special cross-reference system helps you to do this.

Who is *Key Words in Business* for?

Key Words in Business is designed for:

Self-study learners of business English: upper intermediate and advanced learners of English in business contexts working on their own who wish to develop their knowledge of key business vocabulary and how to use it in discussing current business topics.

Business and management English classes and business studies course participants. The book can be used to provide stimulating input to language training in business and management English, and to classes for native speakers on business studies courses. Participants look at key business language and get the opportunity to discuss a wide variety of business issues in relation to their own business backgrounds and interests.

Structure

Each chapter consists of a logical sequence of topic sections. Each topic section contains these parts:

- **Key words and commentary.** The key words in a specific area are listed, explained and defined in relation to each other and in their grammatical context.

- **Examples** from newspapers and business books illustrate the meanings of these key words in context. Most of the extracts are at least one sentence or longer so as to give a good sense of overall context. The examples have been chosen for their intrinsic interest, and for their illustrative and explanatory power.
- **Language activities** further refine understanding of how the key words are used, relate to each other and to other words; develop awareness of grammatical context; and show how the key words fit into overall patterns of meaning. Many of the activities are based on long extracts which can be used for group discussion.

Section content

Key words, commentary, and language notes

Each commentary brings together a number of related key words, explaining and defining them in a continuous text. The key words are indicated in **bold** in the commentary itself and are also listed in logical groups in the shaded box.

Where relevant, the commentary is followed by language notes providing grammatical information about key words in the commentary (where this information is not given in the commentary itself) and giving variations in spelling and hyphenation.

headhunt
headhunter
headhunting

golden hello

Headhunters are specialist consultants who search for high-level, often board-level, executives and try to persuade them to leave their current job in order to go to work in another company. Managers found in this way are **headhunted** in a process of **headhunting**.

Executives may be persuaded to move company by the promise of a **golden hello**: a large sum of money or some other financial enticement offered by the company they move to.

◆ **LANGUAGE NOTE**

Headhunt, **headhunter**, and **headhunting** are also spelled with a hyphen and as two words.

Examples

The examples have been chosen to provide interesting illustrations of how the key words are used. They are in *italics*, and the first occurrence of a key word is *underlined*.

Mr Malpas, 62, was headhunted from BP to take on the chairman's job and is believed to have been on a salary of about £200,000.

Forgan is being recommended for the post of director of corporate affairs by the headhunters employed by the BBC to fill the £120,000-a-year post.

Goddard Kay Rogers, one of the biggest names in the headhunting industry, has found that the search is not so easy when it is closest to home. After some time looking for an American consultant to head its office in New York, it has finally found the right person just up the road in London.

NEW CHIEF AT TROUBLED IBM PICKS UP $5 MILLION 'GOLDEN HELLO'. The new chief of IBM, Louis Gerstner, will earn a basic salary of $2 million a year and receive a one-off payment of $5 million for leaving his present job as chairman of the food and tobacco giant RJR Nabisco.

Cross-referencing

An arrow with a page number in the right-hand margin indicates that a word in the text is defined as a key word in another chapter of the book. (Key words dealt with elsewhere in the same chapter are not indicated in this way.) Likewise, if a key word is defined in two places, either with the same meaning or a different meaning, arrows point to the other occurance.

The gurus call it 'downsizing'. Last year, in an unending quest for lower costs, higher productivity and fatter profits, American firms announced 615,000 job cuts, an all-time record. In the first seven months of 1994, according to Challenger, Gray & Christmas, a Chicago consultancy, a further 319,000 workers suffered the same fate. Altogether, corporate America now spends $10 billion a year on restructuring.

profits 135 ⇓

restructuring 21 ⇑

The cross-reference system is designed to encourage you to browse, following your own routes through the book.

There is also a full index at the back of the book.

Language activities, and hints on how to do them

Each activity gets you to do one of these things, or a combination of them:

◆ **Find a word** missing from a number of different contexts by looking at meaning and grammar.

- **Think about words and their meanings by putting them into an overall context.** Where a list of words is given for gap completion of sentences or a text, read the instructions carefully: some of the words may be used more than once, and some not at all.
- **Match words to their definitions.** Look through all the items before completing the exercise: don't jump to conclusions.
- **Match sentences or sentence-parts** to take meaning, context, and grammar into account. Look specially for clues to help you combine sentence-parts not only meaningfully but grammatically.
- **Re-order sentences and paragraphs** to build logically developed texts, sometimes sorting out extracts from different sources. Read the instructions carefully for clues on which part comes first. Again, look specially for clues to help you combine sections not only meaningfully but grammatically to build up logically developed texts.
- **Read articles and texts** and answer questions designed not only to *test* understanding of key words but also to *develop* this understanding in wider contexts. Look at networks of meaning, reusing the key vocabulary of the chapter, relating it to what you already know. You may need to look up some words in a dictionary, such as the *Collins Cobuild English Dictionary*.
- **Test your knowledge of meaning and spelling of words** in crosswords and word games.

Conventions

Language activities

Where language activities require missing words to be given, a continuous line indicates that the word may be of any length, as here:

> Since Toyota had not got the money to stockpile parts and materials, Mr Ohno evolved the ______________ system by which the products are pulled through the system by market demand, rather than being driven by the supply of raw materials.
>
> *Answer: kanban*

Where spaces are indicated like this, each underlining indicates one missing letter:

> Earnings not distributed are _ _ _ _ _ _ _ _, which may be used to finance a company's development in _ _ _ _ _ _ _ _ _ _ _ _ _ _ _ in investment, or paid out in a later period to shareholders.
>
> *Answers: reserves, capital spending*

'Gift' letters may sometimes be given, like this:

A country's GDP (Gross Domestic Product) is a measure of its w e a _ _ _.

Answer: wealth

Note on sources

Key Words in Business has been developed using text databases containing nearly 100 million words of text from a variety of newspaper and business book sources.

The sources from The Bank of English include:

The Economist. British weekly. Focus not exclusively economic, but also political and cultural. Circulation 500,000, half in the United States.

The Times. Sometimes perceived, perhaps wrongly, as the voice of the British establishment. Circulation 650,000.

Sunday Times. Sister paper to *The Times.* Circulation: 1,200,000.

The Independent. Daily, founded in 1987 to compete in the British quality market, consisting until then of *The Times, The Guardian* and the *Daily Telegraph.* Circulation 300,000.

The Guardian. Left of centre daily. Circulation 400,000.

Wall Street Journal. New York-based daily. Voice of American business. Circulation 1,700,000.

Today. Tabloid format daily, ceased publication in November 1995.

The other main newspaper sources are the *Financial Times,* British-based European newspaper, circulation 300,000; and the *Independent on Sunday,* praised for its business coverage, circulation 300,000.

A database of business journals, magazines, and books, collated and maintained at the School of English, University of Birmingham, has also been used.

1 What business are you in?

Business and businesses

business company firm concern

Business is the production, buying, and selling of goods and services.

goods 84 ⇓
services 85 ⇓

A **business, company,** or **firm** is an organization that sells goods or services.

A business may also be referred to formally as a **concern.**

The business of America is business.

Unless you understand how money flows through a business, you will not understand the operation.

Mr Gates's boyhood pastime was computer programming. Today Microsoft, his company, is the world's most successful supplier of computer software.

Imagine Japan allowing Sony to be the only Japanese firm to make a product like a Walkman.

Du Pont, a chemicals concern based in Wilmington, Del., brings its extensive agricultural research staff to the project.

enterprise free enterprise private enterprise commerce commercial

A business may be referred to approvingly as an **enterprise** to emphasize its adventurous, risk-taking qualities, and business in general may be referred to in the same way, for example in combinations such as **free enterprise** and **private enterprise**.

Business is also referred to as **commerce**. This word, and its related adjective **commercial**, are often used to distinguish the business sphere from other areas such as government or the arts, or to distinguish it from non-money-making activities.

There is now greater emphasis on terms like project and venture, setting up an enterprise that will run for a time and then be sold on.

Americans have an ease with individual enterprise and risk that few Europeans share.

The preservation of a system of free enterprise is essential to economic freedom.

Government in Malaysia has promised to reduce its interference in the economy and rely on private enterprise to pace economic growth.

The government's concern is to ensure that schools are teaching skills which are useful to industry and commerce.

Kangaroo hunting is not just a hobby but a lucrative commercial business.

1 **Business partners.** The words in the box frequently occur after 'business'.

		leaders		
	school		interests	
ventures		**business**		empire
	community		confidence	

Find combinations that mean:

1 an individual's business activities, especially those of politicians.
2 a very large business organization.
3 specific money-making projects, perhaps involving an element of risk.
4 an institution that awards qualifications in business studies.
5 people involved in business in general.
6 heads of important companies who speak for 5 as a whole.
7 the morale of all those referred to in 5 and 6.

From multinationals to small firms

corporation
corporate

multinational

big business

small and medium-sized companies

small business
small firm

Large companies are referred to as **corporations**, especially in the United States.

Corporate is used to describe things relating to a corporation, or to corporations in general, in expressions like the ones in the next exercise.

Large companies operating in many countries are **multinationals**.

Big business can refer to large business organizations or to any business activity that makes a lot of money.

Small companies are referred to as **small businesses** or **small firms**.

Unlike some languages, English does not have an everyday term for **small and medium-sized companies**, apart from this rather clumsy expression.

'This is a rough place – instead of a corporate ladder we have a corporate food chain.'

The South depends more on small and medium-sized businesses for jobs than on large corporations.

The decision was taken to sell BP's three corporate jets.

Some of the operations of a typical multinational are more global than others.

In Korea, democracy has slowed some government decision-making. But it has also cut the power of big business groups and the bureaucracy, in the process creating freer markets and more opportunities for small businesses.

Tourism in Hong Kong is big business: it is the third largest source of foreign exchange and employs, directly and indirectly, 180,000 people.

Women run 25 per cent of existing small businesses, but 33 per cent of new businesses are now started by women.

...the small firm's greatest handicap: not size, but loneliness.

...the south-west of Germany, a haven of small and medium-sized companies, or 'Mittelstand' as they are known.

2 **Corporate partners.** The words in the box frequently occur after 'corporate'.

		image		
	strategy		collapses	
governance		**corporate**		culture
	logo		ladder	
		performance		

Find combinations that refer to:

1 the perception that people have of a corporation.
2 what corporate employees climb during their career.
3 company results over a period of time.
4 the values that people have and the ways that things are done in an organization.
5 the way a company is managed at the highest level.
6 plans that companies have maintaining and developing their position in the future.
7 company failures.
8 a symbol, usually showing the company's name.

Now use these expressions to complete the extracts.

a Corporate ____________ and associated fiascos have exposed the failure of the auditing industry as a whole, not just the failure of individual audits.

b No single subject has so dominated the attention of managers, consultants and management theorists as the subject of corporate ____________ .

c While Wal-Mart grew, Walton was developing the practices that were to give the firm one of America's most-admired corporate ____________s.

d Huet, remaining one step ahead on the corporate ____________ , has been transferred to New York as head of Société Générale in America.

e Good corporate ____________ should be about stopping messes from happening, not just cleaning up afterwards.

f Few investors are prepared to look beyond conventional measures for assessing corporate ____________ .

g All phone books are to have identical blue covers with the British Telecom ____________ . It is part of the corporate ____________ .

3 **Wearing the corporate identity.** Read this article from the *Independent on Sunday* and answer the questions.

CORPORATE IDENTITY: THE EXECUTIVE UNIFORM

An expensive advertising campaign can attract you to a company, its impressive building will make you glad you came, but if the first person you deal with is wearing a purple tank top and flared trousers, are you really going to take them seriously?

A uniform is the most personal manifestation of a company's corporate identity, so companies specialising in 'executive careerwear' are putting white collar workers and professionals into 'corporate suits'.

John Larder, a Midland Bank branch manager, wears his dark blue corporate suit by choice. 'We can choose between single-breasted or double-breasted, and I alternate between the two. However, I wouldn't wear it out if I was with a customer as I think it would be unfair for them to be seen with someone who is obviously a Midland Bank man.'

1 Even if you don't know what a tank top is, does the writer imply that it is a suitable thing for someone working in a company to wear?

advertising campaign *104* ⇓

2 Are white collar workers obliged to wear shirts with white collars in your country, even if they don't wear a uniform provided by the company?

white-collar worker *43* ⇓

There is often a certain amount of choice available in terms of style and colour, so not everyone ends up dressed identically. But together, the effect remains co-ordinated. At the Abbey National not only are corporate suits provided, but the corporate identity is carried into maternity wear and for the special requirements of ethnic groups. ... The majority of people who wear corporate clothing are those who deal directly with the public, and the response from customers has been very positive. ...

But who among the professionals would wear company colours, and how are they persuaded to do so? The most recent newcomers to corporate dressing are financial services companies such as banks and building societies and the challenge is to find a look that pleases everyone. ...

There will always be those who consider that being asked to wear a uniform is a dubious privilege. A senior employee at a leading estate agent says: 'When the clothes were introduced, we were all on the phone to our lawyers because we just didn't want to wear them. Some people even left their jobs.' ...

Chris Willows, of BMW, explained why the company does not have corporate clothing for its sales people. 'One of the linchpins of BMW's philosophy is its individuality, both in the type of product it produces and the type of customer it attracts. We are a company which places tremendous emphasis on corporate identity, even down to the type of tile for the showrooms, but there is a difference between bricks and mortar and a human being.

But even when organisations do not have corporate clothing, they still expect their staff to dress to reflect the company's values. That means saving the purple tank tops for evenings.

3 Another important part of an organization's corporate identity is its l _ _ g _.

4 Is a dubious privilege a privilege that people really want?

5 If X is the linchpin of Y, is X an important part of Y?

6 If you place tremendous emphasis on something, do you think it is unimportant?

7 Would you wear a uniform or 'corporate clothing' to work? If you do already, what do you think of it?

Industries and sectors

industry

sector
- public sector
- private sector
- manufacturing sector
- service sector

Businesses may be classified according to which **industry** they are in: for example construction, oil, banking, food.

Sector is sometimes used to mean industry in the same way, particularly by specialists such as financial journalists, but it is more often used to talk about different parts of the economy in combinations such as **public sector** and **private sector**, or about types of business in expressions like **service sector** and **manufacturing sector**.

market sector 83 ⇓

Arden's customers are primarily in the packaging industry but also the electronics sector.

Many people in the private sector had to take very low pay increases this year.

The French government is thinking of introducing German-style worker participation into the state industries. This suggests that public-sector companies will not be free from political interference, a fact that deters private, profit-minded investors.

One industry that has kept the manufacturing sector going for much of this year is aircraft.

Many young workers are taking jobs in the rapidly growing service sector - banking, computer programming, financial services.

4 Key sector exercise. The same word is missing from all these extracts. What is it?

The report shows about 150,000 jobs were created last month, but some economists expect the	sector to show a net loss of jobs.
The highest number of closures were in the	sector, followed by construction, finance and retail.
Mr Renaud said that in the equipment	sector, Philips would be hardest hit.
... Scottish food and drink, Scotland's biggest	sector, employing 70,000 people.
But with a bit of luck, the worst in the	sector could be over.
In the..............	sector there's evidence that small companies may account for a larger share of the nation's manufactured exports than once thought.
It illustrates the need for a strong	sector if the UK is to maintain growth in living standards.

Public sector and private

nationalized
nationalization
privatized
privatization

state-owned

sell off
sell-off

utilities

When a private company is bought by the state and brought into the public sector, it is **nationalized** in a process of **nationalization**. A nationalized company is **state-owned**.

When the state returns a company to the private sector in a **sell-off**, it is **privatized**. This is **privatization**.

The first to be **sold off** in a privatization programme are often the companies responsible for the public supply of electricity, water and gas: the **utilities**.

'Six of them aren't privatised utility executives.'

◆ **LANGUAGE NOTE**

Privatize, privatization, nationalize, and **nationalization** are also spelled **privatise, privatisation, nationalise,** and **nationlisation** in British English.

British Rail stations worth about £10 billion will be sold off under Government plans to privatise the network.

Malaysia is five years into an initial privatization program. To date, 22 government-owned concerns have been privatized, including a lottery, the national airline and shipping companies, regional water utilities, highway construction projects and a commercial tv station.

Moving even further from the Swedish model, Sweden is to sell 35 state-owned companies. The sell-off could raise as much as $50 billion.

Government intervention in manufacturing investment is a bad joke in every for-God's-sake-let's-privatise-it nationalised industry from Buenos Aires to Omsk.

Mr Salinas has undone two gross acts of confiscation, namely the nationalisation of the banks in 1982. The other was the nationalisation of the oil industry by Lazaro Cardenas in 1938. The oil business is the biggest sacred cow of them all.

5 Unpopular privatizations.

Read this article from *The Economist* and complete it using the words listed. (a occurs five times, b twice, and c and d once each.)

a privatisation c nationalised

b privatised d renationalised

DISGUSTED

Most Britons see privatisation as a rip-off. The evidence says otherwise.

To say that ________ (1) in Britain is unpopular in Britain is an understatement. Every week brings fresh outrage at tales of bosses of ________ (2) firms picking up huge pay rises while over-charging customers, sacking employees and cutting the pay of those who remain. The ordinary man, who has never liked ________ (3), wants the water and electricity industries, and maybe more, to be ________ (4). ...

So what can be said in defence of ________ (5)? Actually a great deal. Back in 1979, Britain's public-sector firms were in the doldrums, lacking both entrepreneurial vigour and a concern for customer service. Many were losing large sums of money. According to the Treasury, the ________ (6) industries were then costing each tax-payer the equivalent of £300 in today's money.

Since ________ (7) - and the changes in management, financial controls and regulation associated with it - these firms have been transformed. Most ________ (8) companies were more profitable in real terms in 1994 than in the year before they were sold. Most had higher sales, and a higher share price than in their first year after ________ (9). They now pay £2.5 billion a year in taxes (equivalent to £100 for each taxpayer). ...

Firms such as British Airways and British Telecom have been turned from corporate dogs into some of the world's most admired companies. ...

entrepreneur 28 ⇓

customer 79 ⇓

Stakes

shares
equity

holding
shareholding
shareholder

stake
- hold a stake
- majority stake
- controlling stake
- minority stake

If Company A owns **shares** or **equity** in Company B, A has or **holds a stake, holding** or **shareholding** in B.

equity 163 ⇓
shareholders' funds 163 ⇓

If A owns less than half the shares in B, it has a **minority stake** in B.

If A owns more than half the shares in B, it has a **majority stake** or **controlling stake** in B.

If you have shares in a company you are a **shareholder**.

One aircraft industry analyst said, 'If GPA is to survive, it must raise more equity from its existing shareholders.'

The Spanish banks have the sorts of links with the corporate world that are typical of the German banks, with the banks holding large stakes in almost all the major Spanish companies. Some of the banks have begun to rethink this situation.

The position of the Fayed brothers, proprietors of Harrods, who have held a 10% shareholding in Sears for years, is becoming very interesting.

The very rich Marc Rich is to retire from the company he founded 15 years ago and will reduce his controlling stake to 15% within five years.

McPherson always takes a majority stake in the businesses he invests in and he likes a hands-on role in the management.

Eurocom has been attempting to raise its minority stake in WCRS's ad business to a majority.

6 **Risky stakes?** Read this article from *The Economist* and answer the questions.

BIOTECH GOES GLITZY

For all the talk about miracle drugs, the biotechnology industry's greatest successes have been financial, not scientific.

Stockmarket investors have sunk $4 billion into the biotechnology industry over the past five years, despite the fact that most biotech firms have yet to show a profit. Now even Wall Street is losing its taste for biotech shares. So the industry's ever-inventive entrepreneurs are concocting a sophisticated range of partnership deals with big companies. Such deals are uncannily similar to the way that independent film producers raise money in Hollywood. Hollywood?

Biotechnologists shudder at the comparison, but there are parallels between the economics of their risky business and that of Tinseltown. Both industries have to spend gigantic sums developing products long before it is clear whether they will cover their costs, let alone make a profit.

Both involve lengthy periods of waiting. A film usually takes five years to pay back its investors, while a drug may take eight years. And both industries rely on a few blockbusters to pay for an enormous number of failures. Thus, less than 10% of the $100 million it took to make Terminator 2 came from the film's producer, Carolco Pictures; the rest came from a cluster of different sources, including Columbia Tri-Star, which distributed the picture to American movie theatres, and Canal-Plus, a French cable-TV company. ...

Many biotech firms are financing their research in a similar way. Joel Marcus, a Los Angeles lawyer who specialises in the biotechnology industry, describes a typical biotech firm as one needing $200 million to bring its first drug to market. Only $80 million of this comes from the sale of shares. Another $20 million is raised by conducting research for other companies. But $100 million comes from a corporate partner, usually a big drug firm. It either pays cash, even

1 Do ever-inventive people have a lot of ideas?

entrepreneur 28 ⇓

2 If X is uncannily similar to Y, is it very like Y?

3 Would biotechnologists approve of this comparison?

4 A blockbuster is a very big s _ c c _ _ _ _.

research 59 ⇓

before a drug is out of the laboratory, or it undertakes to perform the costly chores of testing and manufacturing it in exchange for marketing rights. ...

In 1985, Johnson & Johnson picked up nearly all the marketing rights to three Amgen drugs, including EPO, a treatment for anaemia which has since become a blockbuster. ... Since then Amgen has won ever better, and ever more complicated, deals with its partners. ... Amgen's success reflects the growing clout of biotech firms with the world's biggest drugmakers, who are afraid that the biotech industry will sweep away many of its biggest money-spinners with new, unexpected treatments. Even when a big drug firm buys a controlling stake in a biotech firm, it is usually careful to let the firm's founders continue to run it. When Hoffmann-Laroche bought a 60% stake in Genentech in 1990, it demanded only two of Genentech's 13 board seats. ...

5 A chore is a task, but can it be an easy, pleasant task?

6 Is a blockbuster a money-spinner?

7 People and organizations with clout have a lot of p _ _ e r and i n _ l _ _ _ c _.

8 If you are the founder of something, did you a) find it, or b) found it?

Parents and sisters

holding company
subsidiary
  wholly-owned

parent company
sister company
brother-sister company

group
conglomerate
giant

A **holding** or **holding company** is one that holds stakes in one or more **subsidiaries**. If it owns all the shares in a subsidiary, the subsidiary is a **wholly-owned** one.

A holding company's relationship to its subsidiaries is that of **parent company**, and the subsidiaries' relationship to each other is that of **sister companies**. A holding and its subsidiaries form a **group**.

A **conglomerate** is a group containing a lot of different companies in different businesses. Journalists also refer to large groups as **giants**.

◆ **LANGUAGE NOTE**

Some people reject the term **sister company** as sexist, and refer to **brother-sister companies**.

Newspaper Publishing, the holding company which owns the daily and Sunday Independent titles, announced the plans to increase the Spanish/Italian stake as part of a range of financing options.

Mr Fitzpatrick did not gain control of Goodman Holdings, the Irish-registered parent of the maze of Goodman companies, until last Friday. Goodman Holdings has subsidiaries in Liechtenstein and the Channel Islands, which control investments around the world.

General Motors is, in effect, an 'alliance' in which the principal 'partners' are not merely wholly owned subsidiaries but elements within a single integrated management structure. Toyota is a much looser confederation.

Oakland tries to avoid contracts with companies that it lists as doing business in South Africa. The list covers companies with license agreements, though it still doesn't touch brother-sister companies.

...the personal stereo invented by electronics giant Sony.

The fate of the sportswear company Adidas was decided yesterday. The French businessman Bernard Tapie has sold his controlling stake in the group to a group of investors for DM615 million.

Pearson, a publishing-to-tableware conglomerate that controls the Financial Times, Penguin books and 50% of The Economist, bid for Thames Television, Britain's biggest independent TV producer. Thorn EMI, a music-to-lighting group accepted, agreeing to sell Pearson its 59% stake in Thames for £99 million.

7 **Fingers in many pies.** Which key word in this section is missing, in its plural form, from all these extracts?

in making Airbuses. But Daimler's aerospace	....	, now called Deutsche Aerospace, want to take
Information should flow up the overseas	....	to the parent; decisions would be decentralised
Sun is still trying to work out how to get these	....	to work independently but co-operatively.
Take a multinational company, give it 30	....	, a staff of 50,000 and a budget for its main unit
of firms within Hanson. The use of offshore	....	complicates things further. In 1989 Hanson under
talk of Euro-managers, he expects the group's	....	will continue to be managed largely by locals
South African style, it also owns large stakes in	....	outside mining, which are worth another 9 billion

Launching a bid

take over
takeover
  takeover bid
  takeover target

launch a bid
hostile bid

acquire
make an acquisition

There is excitement when Company X is attempting to gain control of Company Y in a **takeover bid**, perhaps by increasing its holding or stake in company Y if it already owns shares in Y.

Company X makes or **launches a bid** against company Y, the **takeover target**.

If Company Y does not want to be taken over, the bid is **hostile**.

Other ways of saying that one company is **taking over** another are to say that one company is **acquiring** another or **making an acquisition**.

Tokay, the world's oldest wine appellation, is being acquired by a Japanese distiller and a French insurance group.

Medeva, the fast-growing pharmaceuticals group, rose 19p to 224p on the news that it has made another acquisition in America. Medeva is to buy Adams Laboratories, a Texas drugs manufacturer, for $77.2 million.

TT Group, the packaging company, has launched its second hostile takeover bid in little more than a year, with a £6.8 million offer for Magnetic Materials Group, the magnetic components manufacturer. TT won a long running bid battle for Crystalate last August. The 37p share offer is equal to the price paid by TT on Tuesday for a 9.4 per cent stake, bringing its total holding in the target company to 16.2 per cent. This compares with a market price of 41p before and after the announcement of the bid. Magnetic's board rejected the bid as 'derisory, unsolicited, unwelcome, and totally inadequate'.

8 **Bid types.** In the last example above, Magnetic's board rejected TT's bid as 'derisory, unsolicited, unwelcome, and totally inadequate'. Match these adjectives, and others describing takeover bids, to their meanings.

	abortive		unsought
	contested		unwanted
	derisory		fought against
If a bid is	inadequate	it is	insultingly low
	sweetened		not enough
	unsolicited		unsuccessful
	unwelcome		improved

Predators, raiders, and white knights

predator
prey

raider
corporate raider

The takeover process is often described in terms of one animal hunting another: a company or individual seeking to take over another company may be referred to as a **predator**, and the target company as the **prey**.

Predators are also referred to as **raiders** or **corporate raiders**.

The company, and the sector, have deep problems to cope with and an uncertain future ahead. In their present state, they are sitting ducks for European or American predators looking for an entree to the British insurance market.

The group could fall prey to one of the industry's hungrier predators.

Lee Iacocca, Chrysler's boss, explored the possibility of a takeover of General Motors, on behalf of a corporate raider in 1987, but dropped the idea after deciding 'it might be easier to buy Greece'.

fend off a bid
ward off a bid

poison pill

white knight

greenmail

A company wishing to resist, **ward off,** or **fend off** being taken over has a number of options.

It may devise plans that give existing shareholders special rights, or it may make itself less attractive to bidders by selling off a valuable part of the company, or holding on to an unattractive one. Actions like these are **poison pills.**

Or it may persuade a friendly partner, a **white knight**, to take a stake in the company, thus preventing a complete takeover by a hostile bidder.

Bidders may agree to withdraw their bid if paid enough money for the shares they hold in the target company. This is **greenmail.**

The agreement will help Navigation Mixte fend off potential raiders.

London Weekend Television's attempt to attract a white knight to help it ward off the unwanted takeover bid from Granada has collapsed. US West, the giant US telephone company and one of the largest cable operators in the UK, was interested in a stake of 29.9 per cent in the London ITV company - the largest amount possible without triggering a full bid.

UK merchant banks do not appear attractive at the moment. Indeed, TSB's chairman, Sir Nicholas Goodison, perhaps should consider holding on to Hill Samuel: it is a poison pill against predators who might want to swallow the whole group.

... greenmail transactions, in which the target of a takeover attempt buys off the hostile bidder by repurchasing any shares that it has acquired. Greenmail means that these shares are repurchased by the target at a price which makes the bidder happy to agree to leave the target alone.

9 Swallowing the poison pill. Re-arrange these sections from a *Financial Times* article into a logical order. (The first section is a and the last is f.)

TIME WARNER IN ANTI-TAKEOVER MOVE

a Time Warner, the US media group in which Canada's Seagram drinks company has built up an 11 per cent stake, announced yesterday it was introducing a poison pill anti-takeover device which will prevent any investor buying more than 15 per cent of its stock. Seagram, which is controlled by the Bronfman family and began buying Time Warner stock last summer, has announced plans to buy up to 15 per cent of the company's shares for investment purposes.

b Time Warner said it had developed the pill following concern from several institutional investors and the group's strategic partners. Its partners include US West, the Baby Bell regional telephone company, and Japanese companies Toshiba and Itochu, each of which owns a stake in the group's cable and entertainment operations.

c Time Warner is apparently concerned that Seagram's stake could turn out to be unfriendly, though the company yesterday sought to portray the poison pill as a general response to the takeover wave sweeping the US media industry. Mr Gerald Levin, Time Warner's chairman, said yesterday's action 'in no way interferes with Seagram's stated objective to acquire up to 15 per cent of Time Warner's stock as a friendly and supportive investor'.

d Seagram said the move did not appear to interfere with its objectives but added it did not believe poison pills were in the best interests of shareholders, since they could interfere with choice and adversely affect values. The drinks company has no large interests in the entertainment business but Mr Edgar Bronfman Jr, its young president, has dabbled in film production and has expressed enthusiasm for the media industry.

e The scheme is triggered if an investor buys more than 15 per cent of the company's stock. That gives all shareholders - apart from the 15 per cent investor - the right to buy stock at a large discount.

f Time Warner said the pill, known formally as a shareholder rights plan, would not preclude a bona-fide all-cash offer for the company which treated all shareholders equally. It was designed to protect against 'abusive takeover tactics, including acquisition of control without paying all shareholders a fair premium'.

Leveraged buy-outs and junk bonds

leveraged buy-out
LBO

junk bonds

In a **leveraged buyout**, or **LBO**, a company is acquired by a group of investors, often financed by heavy borrowing. The debt is then paid out of the target company's operating revenues or by selling its assets.

debt *128* ⇓

leverage *132* ⇓

The borrowing involved in LBOs is often high-risk debt called **junk bonds**.

bonds *148* ⇓

LBOs financed by junk were frequent in the 1980s and after an absence following the excesses of that period, they are now occurring again.

◆ **LANGUAGE NOTE**

Buy-out is also spelled **buyout**.

'Just Business' explains many business issues usually shrouded in mysticism and emotive language. For instance it made me feel at home with junk bonds for the first time. These are simply fixed-interest securities with less than investment-grade level rating. They are in themselves a borrowing instrument, which are neither good nor bad, but have acquired a bad name because of their use in certain criminal transactions.

An example of a solid company that seems to have thrived on the strength of junk-bond financing is FMC Corp., which makes armored vehicles and other military equipment. In 1986, the company, its shareholders and employees bought out its stock in a leveraged buy-out financed by junk.

10 **Giants and midgets.** Read the above section and the section on leverage in chapter 5. Then complete this extract using the expressions listed. (a occurs four times, c three times and the others once each.)

a junk bonds
b junk bond
c corporate
d equity
e takeovers
f leverage

ACQUISITION VIA JUNK

During the 1980s, new issues of __________ (1) multiplied tenfold as more and more companies issued large quantities of low-grade debt to finance __________ (2) or defend themselves against being taken over. The development of this market for low-grade __________ (3) bonds was largely the brainchild of the investment banking firm Drexel Burnham Lambert.

The result was that for the first time __________ (4) midgets were able to take control of __________ (5) giants, and they could finance this activity by issues of debt. However, issuers of __________ (6) often had debt ratios of 90 or 95 per cent.

Many worried that these high levels of __________ (7) resulted in undue risk and pressed for legislation to ban __________ (8) . Between 1986 and 1988 Campeau Corporation amassed a huge retailing empire by acquiring major department store chains such as Federated Department Stores and Allied Stores.

Unfortunately, it also amassed $10.9 billion in debt, which was supported by just $1 billion of __________ (9). So when in September 1989 Campeau announced that it was having difficulties meeting the interest payments on the debt, the __________ (10) market took a nose-dive and worries about the riskiness of __________ (11) intensified.

Joint ventures and alliances

joint venture

alliance

Two or more companies may decide to work together by setting up a **joint venture** or **alliance** in which each holds a stake.

Lord Weinstock, the managing director of GEC, yesterday for the first time publicly ruled out a takeover bid for British Aerospace and said he would prefer to see joint ventures between the two companies.

Over-the-counter products account for about an eighth of Wellcome sales, but Mr Robb said this did not give the operation sufficient scale. Wellcome would be looking for an alliance or joint venture to boost the business.

11 **Company relationships 1.** Journalists often write about company relationships using the language of courtship, marriage and divorce. Read this article from *The Economist* about a joint venture and complete the definitions below it using words from the article.

LINES ACROSS THE WATER

Britain's telecoms giant, BT, has been unlucky in love. Its courtship of Mintel ended in tears last year, when it sold its stake in the Canadian company at a loss of £120m ($220m). Its agreement with America's McCaw Cellular ended less unhappily with a profit of over £200m. Only a month ago BT's attempts to woo Electronic Data Systems, the world's largest computer-services group, failed. But after an on-off romance, BT leapt into bed with MCI, America's second biggest long-distance telecoms company. 'The telecommunications deal of the century,' says Bert Roberts, MCI's chairman. Ah, but can it last?

The dowry is generous. BT, which has a 95 per cent share of the British market, and MCI are investing a combined $1 billion to launch a new joint-venture company.

1 A man trying to persuade a woman to marry him is said, in old-fashioned English, to _ _ _ her. In the same way, when company A wishes to merge or form an alliance with another company B, A is said to _ _ _ B.

2 Before marriage there is a period of _ _ _ _ _ _ _ _ _ _, and this (again old-fashioned) expression is used to talk about two companies who are discussing the possibility of merging.

3 When it is uncertain whether a marriage is going to take place, commentators talk about an _ _-_ _ _ romance.

4 People who suddenly enter a relationship may be said to _ _ _ _ _ _ _ _ _ _ _ with each other, and the expression is used in the article about two companies who agree to form an alliance.

5 In some cultures, when two people marry, a sum of money called a _ _ _ _ _ is given by one family (usually the bride's) to the other. The article refers to a sum of money to be invested in the joint venture using this word.

6 A relationship between two people that ends unhappily _ _ _ _ _ _ _ _ _ _ _. A joint venture that is abandoned may be referred to in the same way.

12 **Company relationships 2.** The previous article asks if the BT-MCI 'marriage' can last. The next excerpt, from the *Financial Times*, looks at the whole area of strategic alliances. It also uses the language of personal relationships. Match the expressions to their definitions and then use the expressions to complete the article, rearranging the paragraphs into a logical order. (One of the expressions is used twice.)

1	alliances	a	people involved in a sexual or romantic relationship
2	lovers	b	relationships formed between countries or organizations
3	liaisons	c	insect trap known for being very difficult to get out of
4	one-night stands	d	sexual or romantic relationships
5	spider's web	e	relationships lasting only a short time

DANGEROUS ________

a Equally, does IBM really understand where it figures in Toshiba's strategy of ________ with all and sundry? The same applies within the US itself, to IBM's place in Apple's growing ________ of relationships - and vice versa.

b AMD, in its trumpeting of this week's agreement with Fujitsu, seemed to take little account of the Japanese company's extensive network of relationships with western companies, including ICL, Siemens and Amdahl. Does it understand how it features, and could be manipulated, in Fujitsu's global battle against IBM?

c ________ may give companies unprecedented flexibility. But, by the same token, they render them unstable. To revert to analogies from personal life, it is far easier to control one's destiny if one has just a couple of mutually compliant ________ than if one tries to run a series of ever-changing ________ .

Mergers

merge merger

When two companies combine, usually voluntarily, they **merge** in a **merger**.

...Lord McGowan and Lord Melchett, who created ICI 66 years ago by merging Nobel Industries and Brunner Mond in an agreement made on board the liner Aquitania as it sailed from New York to London.

Bibby is getting tough with unwilling Spanish bid target Finanzauto. The agribusiness group has abandoned efforts to sweet-talk the Caterpillar vehicles distributor into a friendly merger and has launched a £75 million bid instead.

13 **Unwilling partners.** Here are two articles about the Renault-Volvo merger proposed during the early 1990s. One comes from the *Wall Street Journal* and was written when the merger was first under discussion. The other comes from the *Financial Times* after the proposed merger had been rejected. Sections from each have been interspersed, but are in the right order. Reconstitute each article.

RENAULT, VOLVO IN 'PRELIMINARY' TALKS: MERGER WOULD CREATE NO. 4 AUTO FIRM

FIRMLY EMBARKED ON NEW STRATEGY - PROFILE: VOLVO

a Stung by mounting global competition, Renault of France and AB Volvo of Sweden are exploring a possible merger that would create the world's fourth largest auto company and the biggest truck maker. Volvo confirmed that it and Renault are in 'preliminary' talks. Government-owned Renault declined to comment except to say that it is actively seeking partners.

b 'Firing on all cylinders.' 'Up to speed again.' 'Back in top gear.' To the relief - and pride - of most Swedes, the motoring metaphors have been flowing thick and fast this year for Volvo, the country's biggest manufacturer. Thanks to a dramatic recovery in profits, memories of the ignominious collapse at the end of 1993 of Volvo's plans to merge with France's Renault have faded fast.

c Neither company would discuss details nor comment on the likely outcome of negotiations. But individuals in both countries said the talks have covered a wide range of options, including collaboration in both car and truck operations and perhaps even a full-scale merger of the two concerns eventually.

d People familiar with the talks emphasized that no immediate agreement is in the offing and that some very formidable corporate and political hurdles would have to be cleared before any alliance takes place. One person said the obstacles to a major alliance may be insurmountable. Industry analysts also were skeptical about a combination of two such disparate vehicle makers.

e Volvo returned a 12-fold growth in pre-tax profits in the first nine months of the year to record a surplus of Skr12.7 billion, on turnover of Skr112.2 billion. Under the energetic Mr Soren Gyll, the chief executive who has emerged as the new dominant figure in Volvo, the company is firmly embarked on a new strategy to focus on its core vehicle-making operations.

f By the end of 1996, it intends to have sold off all its non-core activities, raising a total of some Skr40 billion to finance the future development of cars and trucks. Today, there is a widely-held view in the industry that Volvo Truck Corporation is already in strong shape. At the nine-month stage, worldwide unit truck sales were up 38 per cent at 49,400, delivering a jump in operating profits to Skr2.7 billion.

This cartoon from the Swedish daily *Svenska Dagbladet* shows Pehr Gyllenammar of Volvo, with Louis Schweitzer of Renault clearly in the driving seat. The merger did not take place because Swedish shareholders were worried that the partnership would not be equal.

Restructuring

diversified core business profit centre focus assets non-core assets sell off sell-off spin off spin-off dispose of disposal

A group containing many types of business is **diversified**. A group's basic business activity, perhaps the one it originally started with, is its **core business**.

Separate business activities may be viewed as **profit centres**, each responsible for generating profit.

Businesses are often encouraged to concentrate or **focus** on their core activities and to **sell off, spin off,** or **dispose of** non-essential **assets.** These assets are often referred to as **non-core assets**.

assets 130 ⇓

A sale of assets in this way is referred to as a **sell-off, spin-off,** or **disposal**. A **spin-off** can also refer to a business that has been spun off.

◆ **LANGUAGE NOTE**

Sell-off and **spin-off** are also spelled as one word, especially in American English.

... 3M, a diversified multinational that makes an astonishing 60,000 different products.

Since taking over at Nokia two years ago, Mr Ollila has set about completing the company's transformation from a sprawling industrial conglomerate to a group focused on telecommunications and electronics. More than 60 per cent of group sales is accounted for by its telecommunications divisions.

Plessey's non-telecommunications activities split into 23 businesses, self-contained profit centres, each with a manager bearing full profit responsibility.

profit 135 ⇓

The Adelaide Steamship group yesterday announced plans to sell many of its assets and concentrate on the core business of retailing. The sell-off could include Adsteam's controlling stake in Markheath Securities and its substantial holdings in the Australian wine, timber, food, processing and real estate industries.

TSB has been shedding non-core assets for the last two years to concentrate on its main banking and insurance business.

After a promise to shareholders that it would return to its core photographic and health businesses, Eastman Kodak is to spin off its $4 billion chemical subsidiary, the tenth largest in the United States, by the end of the year.

Mr Simons said he had no plans to sell off large numbers of Gateway stores. 'If there are to be disposals,' he said, 'they will be in handfuls rather than large numbers.'

divest divestment pull out of restructuring rationalization

If a company sells a business, it **divests** itself of that business. **Divestment** refers both to the action of selling a business and to the whole process of selling businesses in this way.

If you **pull out of** a business activity, you abandon it, perhaps as part of a programme of **restructuring** or **rationalization**: reorganizing a business with the aim of making it more efficient and profitable.

◆ **LANGUAGE NOTE**

Rationalization is also spelled **rationalisation** in British English.

Turnover fell by 9 per cent to £1.97 billion mainly because of divestments. The group said a further 17 non-core businesses had been sold during the year, and the disposal programme was now complete.

turnover *114* ⇓

Adia's divestment programme is behind schedule.

The next restructuring move is likely to be the sale of Nokia's 80 per cent holding in Nokia Tyres, a move signalled by Mr Ollila last month.

Mr Araskog ruthlessly hacked back the sprawling ITT empire, not only selling off most of the businesses acquired by Mr Geneen, but even pulling out of the telecommunications business on which the group had been built. Rationalisation, however, did not succeed in transforming ITT's lacklustre financial performance.

14 **Sticking to your knitting.** Read this article from the *Financial Times* and answer the questions.

AFTER THE PARTY, IT'S BACK TO BASICS

Advertising agencies, wiser after the 1980s' binge, have turned the corner.

...From the early 1980s until 1989, Ms Tilbian says the advertising industry was 'one big jamboree. It was acquisitions every month and all in different geographical areas and in different related services'. WPP and Saatchi paid inflated prices for US agencies, acquiring huge debts to fund the acquisitions.

The event that sums up the era was Saatchi's abortive bid for Midland Bank in 1987. 'Everybody talks about the bid as the time when the business was at its maddest,' says one

1 If you have a binge, you do things to e _ c _ s _ .

advertising *104* ⇓

2 Do people have a good time when there's a jamboree?

3 If you pay an inflated price for something, do you get value for money?

4 Did Saatchi's bid for Midland succeed? Which two expressions in this paragraph indicate this?

industry observer. 'Its delusions of grandeur were such that, as a simple service business, it could bid for one of the clearing banks, and actually expect to be taken seriously. And for a moment it was.' Midland, roughly twice as big as Saatchi, rejected the idea out of hand. ...

Unlike the recession of a decade ago, the 1990s downturn sank many in the sector. Saatchi and WPP are only now getting debts down to manageable proportions. From having operating margins of a high of more than 13 per cent in the peak year of 1988, Saatchi reached a trough of 2.3 per cent three years later. The broad thrust of the restructuring at both Saatchi and WPP has been to cut jobs, reduce costs and sell non-core businesses acquired during the jamboree.

These moves, combined with the more recent increases in revenues, should bring margins at both groups back up to 10 per cent by 1996. Given these signs of advertising's recovery, could the whole giddy process of boom and bust start again? No chance, is the consensus. For a start, advertisers have learnt certain lessons during the lean times which they will want to continue to apply.

Finally, Ms Tilbian of S G Warburg Securities, argues that, this time round, agencies will be forced to 'stick to the knitting'. No more will they be able to persuade the City that the dreaded word 'synergy' has any meaning in the sector. It was synergy which was supposed to have justified the binge of acquisitions by agencies of management consultancies, public relations firms, recruitment agencies - and even Saatchi's assault on banking.

The synergies proved illusory and many of the businesses have since been sold off. 'At the end of the day you're as strong as your weakest link when you try to sell all your services to your clients,' says Ms Tilbian. 'If one of them botches up, then you could lose your most valued business. For advertising, it's back to basics.'

5 If you have delusions of grandeur, are you less important than you think you are?

6 If you reject an idea out of hand, do you consider it for a while?

recession 178 ⇓

downturn 176 ⇓

7 In which sense is 'sector' used here? How does this differ from other ways of using the word discussed earlier in this chapter?

peak 176 ⇓

trough 180 ⇓

8 If you give the broad thrust of something, do you go into details?

revenues 114 ⇓

9 Is a giddy process a slow-moving one?

10 Lean times are times of r e c _ _ _ _ _ _ _.

11 If a company 'sticks to its knitting' what does it do?

12 Do people like hearing dreaded words?

13 What assault on banking?

14 If someone botches up, they make a bad m _ _ t _ k _.

Management buy-outs

management buy-out
MBO

venture capital

When a group is restructured, the managers of a business that is to be sold off may want to buy it themselves in a **management buy-out** or **MBO**, usually in combination with an organisation providing finance in the form of **venture capital**.

'You'll be pleased to know I'm using this for venture capital.'

◆ **LANGUAGE NOTE**

Buy-out is also spelled **buyout**.

RJB Mining was the subject of a management buy-out last year that left Mr Budge and other directors in control of 25% of the equity, with the remainder in the hands of venture capital groups led by Schroders.

15 **MBO story.** Re-arrange the sections from this *Financial Times* article into a logical order. (The first paragraph is a and the last is e.)

THE MOST IMPORTANT DEAL OF YOUR LIFE

a The process of raising money for a management buy-out involves managers in the most important deal of their lives. Few will have relevant previous experience. Here is a version of how a deal might evolve and be structured and how it might turn out for the venture capitalists and the MBO team. David Mann knew something was up when he saw his boss's car in the company parking lot. As managing director of Wigits, the engineering subsidiary of Publico Ltd, he would have expected notice of a visit from head office.

b As he hurried along the corridor to his finance director, he wondered why the normally amiable Suit had been so abrupt. Could it be because he would be left out of the deal? Or was it because the sale of Wigits would shrink Suit's empire? His reverie was ended when he nearly collided with Alan Counter, the finance director. 'Alan, great news - we've been given the opportunity to mount an MBO - call the accountants,' Mann said.

c A week later, after a series of preliminary meetings, Mann and his team were sitting in the offices of Grapple Ventures, an investor in MBO teams which had kept particularly close to Wigits's local accountant.

d He soon unravelled the mystery. 'Good news and bad news, David,' said Andrew Suit, group planning supremo, tetchily. 'The board's been persuaded by some damned institution that Wigits doesn't fit in our corporate strategy. I don't agree, but there you are. You have three weeks to mount a management buy-out or the board will offer the company in an auction. Keep in touch.' Mann's jaw fell as Suit swept past him to the car park. Wigits's five-strong executive team had often dreamed about an MBO. But now it was thrust upon them Mann knew they had no idea where to begin.

e The tension was palpable. While Mann needed Alan Counter in preparatory meetings because of his knowledge of the figures, Grapple had just brought him bad news. While he was a fine subsidiary finance director when it came to dealing with a head office, his skills would not be relevant or appropriate when Wigits had its own shareholders and was heading for a flotation. Grapple had concluded it would need to bring in a new finance director.

Crossword

Across

1 Large organization often described as 'sprawling' (12)
4 If two organizations combine as equals, they ______________ (5)
5 Companies getting rid of unwanted subsidiaries ______________ them off (4)
6 This can be either minority or majority (5)
7 Firms attracting unwanted bids ______________ them off (4)
9 A very large concern (5)
10 Companies getting rid of unwanted subsidiaries also ______________ them off (4)
11 Potential raider on the prowl (8)
12 An offer that shareholders may or may not refuse (3)
15 If you have more than 50% of a company's shares, you normally have ______________ of it (7)
16 These can be big or small (5)
17 These can be blocks of shares or companies (8)

Down

1 Could be on its own or part of a group (7)
2 A 1 down that works across borders (13)
3 See 15 down
8 Partnerships (9)
9 The raider's mail may be this colour (5)
13 A subsidiary may be wholly- or partly-owned by its ______________ company (6)
14 This word often follows sell, ward, and spin (3)
15, 3 Don't divest these, whatever you do (4, 6)

2 People and organizations

Suits

businessman
businesswoman
businesspeople

suits

People of all sorts work in business, and the terms **businessman** and **businesswoman** reflect this, referring as they do to a wide range of individuals, from the rich and famous right through to small company owners, from people in large organizations to those who work for themselves.

Businessmen and women are referred to together as **businesspeople**.

When supposedly more 'creative' types such as writers or actors deal with businesspeople, they may refer to them, informally and slightly insultingly, as **suits**.

◆ **LANGUAGE NOTE**

Businessman, businesswoman and **businesspeople** are also spelled with hyphens or as two words.

The French businessman Bernard Tapie has sold his controlling stake in Adidas to a group of investors for DM615 million.

stake 9 ⇑

She was a successful businesswoman, with her own secretarial agency.

Local networks of small businessmen helped people to find work.

Business people make decisions that they don't get feedback on until next year – if then.

If you knew even a little about advertising, you would identify David Abbott at once as a highly-paid 'creative' – possibly a copy-writer – rather than an account-managing 'suit'. But he does wear suits – expensive ones, sometimes striped ones – so you would conclude, again accurately, that he was probably an agency head.

advertising 104 ⇓

1 Types of business people. Find combinations in the box that refer to business people who...

1 are well-known. (2 expressions)
2 have great ability to change things.
3 have been good at their jobs and made money.
4 are important in the place where their business is, but not nationally.
5 are from abroad.
6 own businesses that are not large.

		prominent		
	local		small	
leading		**business people**		foreign
	successful		powerful	

◆ **LANGUAGE NOTE**

The superlative is not used with **leading**. You cannot talk, for example, about 'the most leading business people'.

Now use the words in the box to complete the extracts, choosing between the suggestions in brackets. Each word is used once.

a Many ____________ business people consider it a compliment for an expatriate to be able to converse in their language. (prominent / foreign / small)

b Alison Knight, a ceramic artist, found herself becoming a ____________ businesswoman when she needed factory floorspace to lay out the tiles she had agreed to make for an architect working on a pop star's swimming pool. (small / foreign / powerful)

c All the management techniques we use in business, they knew already. They would be very ____________ business people in their own right. (successful / local / leading)

d Other help to businesses comes from our Training and Enterprise Councils, run by local business people who understand ____________ needs. (foreign / local / successful)

e ...Mr de Benedetti, one of Italy's most ____________ businessmen. (foreign / prominent / leading)

f The Duke should start an appeal to save Rolls-Royce for Britain and encourage ____________ businessmen to drive the cars. (leading / local / powerful)

g Only the most ____________ businessmen, like Mr Ambani, can cut through the red tape by going straight to the top. (powerful / small / leading)

Entrepreneurs and tycoons

entrepreneur
start-up

magnate
mogul
tycoon

An **entrepreneur** is usually someone who builds up a company from nothing: a **start-up** company.

Entrepreneurs may one day become **tycoons, magnates** or **moguls:** rich and successful people with power and influence who head big organizations, usually ones they have built up themselves and in which they have a large personal stake.

stake *9* ⇑

◆ **LANGUAGE NOTE**

The adjective corresponding to **entrepreneur** is **entrepreneurial**. Both words are used showing approval.
Start-up is also spelled **startup** in American English.

I never wanted to be an entrepreneur. I just wanted to be a magazine editor but then I had to make sure that the magazine survived. Since then I have just gone into new businesses that interest me and because I like a challenge.

We're going to make Dataproducts more focused, more like a start-up company, more entrepreneurial in nature.

focus *21* ⇑

Taikichiro Mori, 88, a property tycoon, overcame falling property prices to remain the world's richest individual with a fortune of $13 billion.

...the increasingly far-reaching empire of the Italian media magnate Silvio Berlusconi.

Fidelis Schlee is a publishing mogul and one of the richest men in the Czech Republic. He owns two daily newspapers.

2 Entrepreneurial combinations. Match the two parts of these extracts.

1 Business history books are full of entrepreneurial
2 EDS has turned its relationship with General Motors to advantage despite initial concerns that its entrepreneurial
3 His company, Soria Natural SA, has become an entrepreneurial
4 It was his entrepreneurial
5 Most governments now believe self-employment is something to be promoted and encouraged with tax-payers' money. It releases people's entrepreneurial
6 Mr Azoff was eager to return to a more entrepreneurial
7 The nature of the company and its success since its start-up were closely influenced by the entrepreneurial

a culture would be strangled by GM's bureaucracy.
b firms that failed to survive for long after their founders' departure.
c flair of the founder of the organization, Michael Wood.
d role in which he had a big financial stake in his own efforts. 'I'd rather build a company than run one.'
e skills and is a vital source of new jobs, they claim.
f spirit which took him from being a waiter at the Savoy to riches beyond most people's dreams.
g success story and one of the area's leading employers.

Managers and executives

manager
executive
exec

senior manager
senior executive
top manager
top executive

A **manager** is someone in a position of responsibility in an organization. An **executive** is usually a manager at quite a high level. Executives are also **execs**, an informal expression.

People at the head of an organization are **senior executives** or **senior managers**, **top executives** or **top managers**.

Among other topics included in the conference will be how to handle journalists who discover a top executive has been involved in a scandal.

Mr Perot wanted GM's managers to learn their business by working alongside the people who actually make cars, which is what the top managers of Japan's car firms do.

Thinking and judging preferences are disproportionately found as personality traits among corporate senior managers and executives.

...the florid men who work mid-town: advertising execs from Ogilvy and Mather and journalists from the New York Times.

advertising *104* ⇓

3 Executive exercise. Which of the words in the box is missing from all the extracts? (The word is plural in two of the extracts.)

		pay		
	duties		assistant	
jet		**executive**		stress
	toy		search	

Many looked on the idea of a computerised wallet more as an executive	than a serious business aid.
Where portable computers may previously have been regarded as a status symbol or even as an executive	they are now viewed more objectively and critically by the companies that buy them in quantity.
The group has produced not a breakthrough for medical science and technology, but a £300 executive	and a place in the *Guiness Book of Records.*
Taking the pocket machine back to the office and plugging into the desktop PC is such a chore that most owners of these executive	hardly ever do it.
Image, a chain of shops specialising in pricey executive	, lost money for the first time in 15 years.

Ladies and gentlemen of the board

board of directors

The people legally responsible for a company are its **board** or **board of directors**.

There is no one answer for all companies at all times. It's up to the board of that company to decide how to run the company and for the shareholders to shout if they don't like it. It's important to have a good strong board of directors so they can stand up and say, 'Hang on, you can't do that,' which mine do often.

'If you two are in favor, why don't you raise your hands?'

4 Role-playing. Read the extracts below and complete the commentary.

chairman
chairwoman

managing director
chief operating officer
chief executive
chief executive officer
CEO

The person who chairs board meetings is the __________ or __________ . The position is often combined with that of __________ __________ , who may be responsible for the day-to-day running of the company. This responsibility is made specific in the titles __________ __________ , __________ __________ __________ , or CEO.

Some companies also have a __________ __________ __________ in addition to or instead of a CEO.

Louis Gerstner yesterday took up the most daunting challenge in corporate America when IBM named him as its new chairman and chief executive officer. The 51-year-old chairman of RJR Nabisco will become only IBM's sixth CEO and the first outsider to lead the company in its 79-year history.

...Mr Sugar, the founder, chairman and managing director of the troubled electronics group Amstrad.

Mr Garuzzo was given responsibility for car production in 1990 and last year became chief operating officer, co-ordinating all of Fiat's industrial sectors.

president
vice-president

In the US, the head of a company may have the title **president**. Again, the responsibilities of this post vary from company to company, and the post may be combined with another.

In the US, a senior manager in charge of a function may have the title **vice-president** and may be on the board. One vice-president may have responsibility for running the company, or maybe not, as the last example below indicates only too well.

After a short hiatus, Sandra Kurtzig has returned as chairwoman of ASK Computer Systems Inc. Ms Kurtzig, the founder of this maker of management-information software systems, also will assume the duties of president and Chief Executive Officer.

Federal Express's marketing vice-president, Mike Glenn, says: 'We built the overnight category.'

A spokesman said Mr Roberts had been fired by Arby's board for insubordination and for failing to follow policies and procedures, including using the titles president and chief executive officer when he was only an executive vice president and chief operating officer.

directors
executive
non-executive

Executive directors on a board are high-level managers of the company. Other directors are **non-executive directors**, perhaps bringing their knowledge and experience to several company boards.

Dr Hornsell describes a survey which was done to monitor the executive directors' concepts of the role of the non-executives on his board. The presence of the non-executives made them feel more secure.

5 The Good Board Guide. Read this review of a book about company boards and answer the questions.

'Under the new business, Mr Chambers announced he was retiring as President effective December 31st. A power struggle ensued lasting nearly 45 minutes from which Mr Watkins, bruised, battered but smiling, emerged the victor.'

THE CORPORATE BOARD

The ten largest organisations in the world (by number of employees) are responsible, directly and indirectly, for the welfare of around 20 million people, close to the combined populations of Scandinavia, and their total financial assets amount to $560 billion, more than the combined GDP of Scandinavia and equivalent to that of Canada. Are their board structures and capacities equal to the enterprises they govern?

This question forms the springboard for a stimulating book assessing board practice and structure in Britain, Germany, France, Finland, The Netherlands, Switzerland, Canada and Venezuela.

The authors, both Swiss academics with wide experience of international

1 Someone's welfare is their h___th, com___t, and pros______.
2 A country's GDP (Gross Domestic Product) is a measure of its wea____.
3 Is the way companies are run usually referred to as
a) corporate government, or
b) corporate governance?

assets *130* ⇓
GDP *173* ⇓

companies write elegantly (a distinct bonus in such a book) and are liable to quote such unexpected sources as F Scott Fitzgerald ('The test of a first-rate intelligence is the ability to hold two opposed ideas in mind at the same time and still retain the ability to function.') and the 17th-century Queen Christina of Sweden ('In the art of governing, one always remains a student.') It makes a change from Machiavelli, or for that matter, Peters and Waterman.

The book covers in-depth the role of the board, its structure and balance and the evaluation of board performance, based on a survey of 71 companies and their directors. Much of the experience is common across national cultures and differing types of board. There is no dispute, for example, on the four factors that help to build a board's collective strength:

1 The personality and style of the chairman and CEO, including the structure of the chairman/CEO roles.

2 The culture and climate of board meetings (whether openness and frankness are encouraged or discouraged, the size of the board, how decisions are made and the agenda set, relationships among directors).

3 The people involved, the composition of the board and how directors come to be on the board.

4 The degree of common purpose, the clarity directors experience about their roles.

There is a useful section on the combination or otherwise of the chairman/CEO roles. One British non-executive director (unnamed) suggests that the roles should be separated for continuity's sake, pointing out that when Watergate broke over his head, President Nixon was at the same time head of state and head of government. There was no opportunity to carry on 'above the fray'. ...

4 Why is elegant writing 'a bonus' in this type of book?

5 Why do Fitzgerald and Christina make a change from Machiavelli, and Peters and Waterman? Who are all these people?

6 If there is no dispute about something, do people agree about it?

7 The structure of the chairman/CEO roles refers to the r e l a t i o n _ _ _ _ between them.

8 The climate of a meeting is its a t m o s _ _ _ _ _ _ .

9 If you do something for the sake of something, do you do it for that thing?

10 If you there is a dispute and you are above the fray, are you involved in the dispute?

Headhunting

'How do you do, sir?
My name is John L. Flagman,
and I run a successful executive
search firm.'

headhunt
headhunter
headhunting

golden hello

Headhunters are specialist consultants who search for high-level, often board-level, executives and try to persuade them to leave their current job in order to go to work in another company. Managers found in this way are **headhunted** in a process of **headhunting**.

Executives may be persuaded to move company by the promise of a **golden hello**: a large sum of money or some other financial enticement offered by the company they move to.

◆ **LANGUAGE NOTE**

Headhunt, headhunter, and **headhunting** are also spelled with a hyphen and as two words.

Mr Malpas, 62, was headhunted from BP to take on the chairman's job and is believed to have been on a salary of about £200,000.

Forgan is being recommended for the post of director of corporate affairs by the headhunters employed by the BBC to fill the £120,000-a-year post.

Goddard Kay Rogers, one of the biggest names in the headhunting industry, has found that the search is not so easy when it is closest to home. After some time looking for an American consultant to head its office in New York, it has finally found the right person just up the road in London.

NEW CHIEF AT TROUBLED IBM PICKS UP $5 MILLION 'GOLDEN HELLO'. The new chief of IBM, Louis Gerstner, will earn a basic salary of $2 million a year and receive a one-off payment of $5 million for leaving his present job as chairman of the food and tobacco giant RJR Nabisco.

6 **Ruthless tactics?** Read this article from the *Financial Times* about the headhunting profession, and answer the questions.

POACHER TURNED TV STAR – DO HEADHUNTERS DESERVE THEIR BBC IMAGE?

Last night's episode of *Headhunters*, a new BBC drama, does not present the trade in its most flattering light. Hall works for one of London's foremost headhunting firms, where he spends his time on the mobile phone in constant search of bodies to 'poach'. A client wants to hire an entertainment lawyer: Hall does better by persuading him to poach a whole team. When the head of the old law firm finds out that his valuable assets are about to leave he is so upset he kills himself.

assets

130 ⇓

1 What is normally 'poached' and from where?

Headhunters have never been the most respected profession, but the message from the BBC seems to be that their ruthless tactics are pushing them to new depths of unpopularity.

2 If you use ruthless tactics, do you consider the feelings of other people? Does 'ruthless' show approval or disapproval of these tactics?

Tim Clark, an expert on headhunters at the Open University, argues that the business does not deserve a bad name. He says that from the beginning people have viewed headhunting as a secretive, underhand business, disliking the process by which individuals are approached discreetly and persuaded to move jobs. 'It's an easy industry to pick on. So much of the business is confidential. People don't know the full facts.'

3 If you describe an activity as underhand, do you approve of it?

4 If X picks on Y, is Y able to defend himself or herself properly?

So what are the facts? Is there a moral problem with poaching? Might it be the responsibility of the headhunter to think about the mess that a person leaves behind when they change jobs?

'The work is very sensitive,' says Ian Butcher of Whitehead Mann. 'You can create problems if you take out key people. But most senior businessmen recognise that that is part of the game. In any case, our loyalty is to the client.' ...

5 Does Ian Butcher sympathize with the companies that he persuades people to leave?

Executive pay

'The company lost $76 million last year – do you really think cutting my pay is going to get it all back?'

'What are the stockholders complaining about? I'm making less than a star baseball player.'

compensation
compensation package
remuneration
remuneration package

bonuses
benefits
perks

share options
stock options

When talking about executive pay, **compensation** can refer, confusingly, to two different things:

- what top executives get for running a company.
- what they get on leaving a company.

Apart from salary, an executive's **compensation package** can include:

package 108 ⇓

bonuses: extra payments, sometimes, but not always, related to the firm's performance.

benefits and **perks** ranging from **share options**, the right to buy the company's shares at an advantageous price, to a chauffeur-driven car.

shares 147 ⇓

Remuneration is also used to talk about executives' salary and benefits.

◆ **LANGUAGE NOTE**

Share options are also called **stock options**, especially in American English.

Shareholders have been pressing IBM to split the office of chairman and chief executive officer, to establish independent committees to review company leadership and strategy, and to nominate directors and link executive compensation to IBM's share price.

When Salomon suffers, the shareholders bear the brunt of the poor performance through a lower share price and dividends, while the managing directors are cushioned by compensation packages that are generous enough to ensure Salomon's pay remains competitive.

Most executives value salary increases far more than perks when changing jobs, says a survey carried out by a leading recruitment company. Responses in a recent survey of 146 executives found that 63 per cent of them said they would prefer to have the equivalent increase in salary instead of some or all of the perks on offer. The benefits they considered most important were non-contributory pensions, company cars and healthcare.

Britain's bosses ranked 14th in the international league for salaries and bonuses but in terms of total remuneration they were fifth.

Jerry Garbut said the shares sold were acquired in January by exercising options that were part of their total remuneration package.

7 **Model execs?** Read this article from the *Financial Times* and answer the questions.

WEALTH ELUDES THE SALARYMAN – WESTERN MANAGERS ARE UNDER ATTACK FOR BEING GREEDY. IT'S A DIFFERENT STORY IN JAPAN

By Michiyo Nakamoto

A few years ago, Yutaka Kume, chairman of Nissan, acquired a small, ready-built house, of what might be considered modest proportions, in the outskirts of Tokyo. A photograph of Kume's dream home, sitting on an undistinguished plot of land, shocked the Japanese public when it appeared in a popular magazine.

Expensive as Japanese land prices might be, Kume's residence, located in a distinctly middle-class residential area, was not what might have been expected to be fit for the chairman of Japan's second-largest auto maker. ...

Like Kume, many Japanese executives live in residences which would be considered humble by western standards. And unless they are self-made millionaires, or have inherited wealth, their personal fortune is likely to be so insignificant that it would make American and European executives blush at the comparison.

1 If something eludes you, do you find it easy to obtain?

2 Were the public shocked because the house looked
a) too luxurious, or
b) not luxurious enough?

3 Would American and European executives envy their Japanese counterparts?

According to a survey last year by the Seikei Kenkyu-jo, a private research organisation, the average annual income including bonuses of the presidents of 46 companies listed in the first section of the Tokyo Stock Exchange was ¥37.25m (£223,000). Although this is about 10.5 times the average pay of first-year salarymen, according to the Seikei Kenkyu-jo, it is a paltry sum compared with the millions of dollars paid in remuneration to the executives of America's top corporations.

4 Is a paltry sum a large amount?

One reason for the low level of executives' remuneration is that, unlike western companies, Japanese businesses which use a seniority-based employment system do not make as much of a distinction between ordinary employees and those with executive status. 'In Japan, the executive's job is seen as an extension of the work of other employees, so it is considered inappropriate to create a huge gap between executives' and other employees' pay,' explains Sadao Ohta, director of Seikei Kenkyu-jo. ...

5 If something is inappropriate, is it suitable?

Nor do Japanese companies offer benefits to executives on the basis of performance, such as in the form of preferred shares or stock options which are commonly used in the west. Stock options have made many a businessman in the west quite wealthy. But in Japan, where companies cannot buy their own shares, no such system exists.

6 Wealthy is a fairly formal word for _ _ _ _ .

At the same time, the Japanese company executive is expected to set a good example for other employees. Extravagance in any form is likely to be frowned upon and would trigger criticism at the first signs of a business downturn or unhappiness among employees. So while many would sympathise with Kume, his self-restraint, according to one industry official, 'is a model for the Japanese salaryman'. That role of the company executive, as a mirror for other employees,

7 Extravagant people spend an e _ _ _ _ _ i v e amount of money.

8 If something is a model, are people expected to follow it?

has been in particular evidence during the country's present economic downturn. When business is low it is common practice in Japan for companies to cut executive bonuses and pay first. ...

Executives at Toyota, for example, have had their remuneration cut by 30 per cent since the summer of 1992 while those at Nippon Steel have been living with on average 10 per cent less of their pay since October of that year. To add to their financial woes, Japanese executives are still expected to attend countless weddings, funerals and other social events, and make cash gifts befitting their high social status. However, there are some remuneration compensations. The Japanese executive does generally enjoy round-the-clock use of the company car and his own chauffeur, as well as membership of the most exclusive golf clubs, an entertainment allowance that is almost unlimited and other perks. ...

downturn *176* ⇓

9 Woe is a fairly formal word for w _ r _ y.

10 Is compensation being used here in the way defined in the commentary at the beginning of this section?

Executive pay-offs

golden boot
golden goodbye
golden handshake
golden parachute

compensation payment
compensation payoff
compensation payout

severance package
severance payment

oust

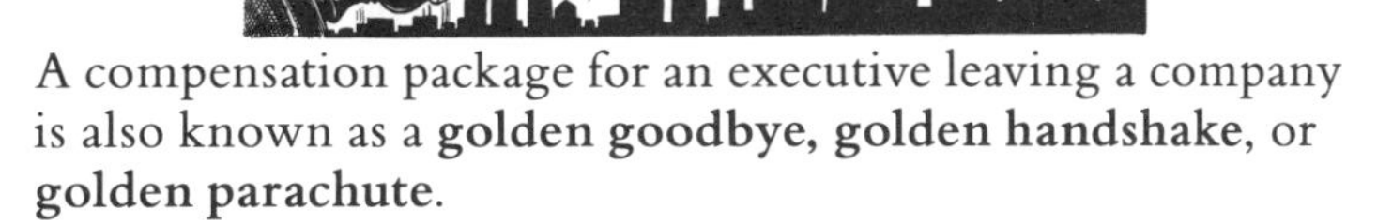

A compensation package for an executive leaving a company is also known as a **golden goodbye, golden handshake**, or **golden parachute**.

Compensation for someone leaving a company may be referred to as a **compensation payment, compensation payoff**, or **compensation payout**.

These payments may form part of a **severance package**.

Severance payments can be the subject of complex negotiations when an executive leaves, or is **ousted**: forced to leave.

When executives are ousted, people may talk about companies giving them the **golden boot**.

◆ **LANGUAGE NOTE**

Payoff and **payout** are also spelled **pay-off** and **pay-out**.

Stephen Walls, who picked up a six-figure golden handshake when Plessey was bid for four years ago, is in line for another bumper pay-off. He stands to receive at least £825,000 compensation after a boardroom row at Anglo-French paper group Arjo Wiggins.

He also said he would work without a contract indefinitely. Such a move would prevent him from receiving substantial 'golden parachute' severance pay should he leave United's employment.

Mr Peter Davis, former co-chairman of Reed Elsevier, the Anglo-Dutch information and publishing group, is to receive one of the largest executive pay-offs in Britain in recent years – a compensation package worth £2.02 million. Mr Davis, who resigned in June after a dispute over management responsibilities, is to receive £652,000 in cash, £1.3m of enhanced pension entitlements and up to £70,000 in fringe benefits, including temporary use of an office suite in London's West End.

Huge payoffs recently have included £1.5 million for Robert Horton, who was ousted as chairman and chief executive of BP following a boardroom row.

International Business Machines gave a 'golden boot' to Mr John Akers, its former chairman and chief executive, who retired last April under pressure from the board of directors as a result of the company's worsening financial performance. According to a statement issued today, Mr Akers received a severance package of about $3.4 million. This included $2.5 million, equivalent to one year's compensation, as part of a retirement incentive programme.

8 Failure-related pay. Complete this extract from *The Economist* using grammatically appropriate forms of the words listed. One of the words is not used.

boot	oust	goodbye	pay-off
compensation	fortune	package	executive

A RACKET IN NEED OF REFORM

Many of Britain's company chiefs are overpaid, including some of the ones being ________ (1) out of their jobs. Other bosses deserve more.

'If you can meet with triumph and disaster and treat those two imposters just the same.' Kipling's test of manhood is proving all too easy for the bosses of British firms: they earn a fortune if they do well, and a ________ (2) if they do badly.

This month, Peter Davis, the departing co-chairman of Reed Elsevier, a publishing firm, carried a ________ (3) worth £2 million ($3 million) away with him in his briefcase; four directors quitting Tiphook, a financially troubled transport firm that lost £331 million last year, have shared ________ (4) of around £4 million; and Peter Sherlock has resigned as chief executive of NFC, a road haulage firm, with a ________ (5) expected to top £750,000 – two years after his hasty exit from Bass, a brewer, with a £395,000 farewell.

Such 'golden ________ (6)', together with massive pay rises for many bosses keeping their jobs, have made ________ (7) pay a political issue. ...

Numbers people

bean-counter
number-cruncher

rocket scientist

Business organizations obviously need people who are good with numbers and computers.

People refer, slightly offensively, to accountants and other numerate specialists as **bean-counters** or **number-crunchers**.

Rocket scientists are people with advanced qualifications in mathematics and related subjects recruited by financial institutions to work on new and extremely complex financial products.

'Before computers and word processors, we were nerds with slide rules and very sharp pencils.'

◆ **LANGUAGE NOTE**

Bean-counter and **number-cruncher** are also spelt as two words.

The reason for America's failure in robots is that we have bean-counters running our companies. The Japanese have engineering and manufacturing people.

Do we want these statisticians and number crunchers to reveal everything about us?

Over the past few years, the financial institutions have recruited mathematicians and physicists – known in the City as 'rocket scientists' – on an unprecedented scale. The Midland team, for example, includes two people who really are rocket scientists; the others have degrees and doctorates in physics, mathematics and engineering.

9 Rocket fuel for banks. This article is from the *Financial Times*. Re-arrange the sections into a logical order. (The first section is a.)

ROCKET SCIENTIST WITH A BILLION-DOLLAR BRAIN

a Derivatives, the complex financial instruments which Flavio Bartmann designs and sells, earned his US investment bank $753m in revenue last year. The trading floor by his office at Merrill Lynch's London headquarters is packed with traders selling forwards, futures, options, swaptions and all manner of financial exotica. Bartmann has only one regret about the way his working life has evolved.

derivatives *154* ⇓

b They have changed the atmosphere of trading floors. While the archetypal trader of the 1980s was the brash, aggressive bond salesman, they are a quieter, more introverted breed. One investment banker tells of wandering past a room in which derivatives traders were discussing mathematical formulae. 'It was like Re-Union Of The Nerds,' he says. ...

techno-nerd *60* ⇓

c 'A year ago, I was flying to New York with my boss,' says the 41-year-old Brazilian, 'and he asked me if I could start again, would I choose this job, or being a professor at Harvard? I said I would take Harvard.' As he talks, derivatives traders tap at rows of computers so sophisticated that they are coveted by university mathematics departments. Bartmann, a former assistant professor of statistics at Columbia University in New York, is what old-fashioned bankers call a 'rocket scientist'. They are people with advanced degrees and doctorates in mathematics, statistics, even astrophysics, who have been lured in their hundreds by banks in Wall Street and the City of London.

d They need mathematical knowledge and ease with computer models because the financial products they sell are so complicated that only mathematicians can calculate the inherent risks. If a bank miscalculated these risks badly, and sold billions of dollars worth of contracts that went wrong, its capital could be wiped out by having to pay the bill. ...

e Yet banks continue to pour money into recruiting rocket scientists to design derivatives. ... The demand for this expertise means that US universities, from which most of the cleverest traders are drawn, have little chance of paying enough to retain them. An average swaps trader in London made between £140,000 and £280,000 last year. The best rocket scientists earn far more: at Merrill Lynch about 10 derivatives specialists are thought to have been paid more than $1m in 1993. ...

Management and labour

staff
employee
workforce
personnel
payroll

shopfloor

white-collar
blue-collar
management
labour

People working for a company are referred to as its **workforce, employees, staff**, or **personnel** and are on its **payroll**.

In some contexts, especially more conservative ones, employees and workforce refer to those working on the **shopfloor** of a factory actually making things. Similarly, staff is sometimes used to refer only to managers and office-based workers.

This traditional division is also found in the expressions **white-collar** and **blue-collar**.

Another traditional division is that between **management** and **labour**.

◆ **LANGUAGE NOTE**

Shopfloor and **workforce** are also spelled with hyphens and as two words.
White-collar and **blue-collar** are also spelled as two words. In American English they may also be spelled as one word.
Labour is spelled **labor** in American English.

Milan city council hires the opera's manager and all the 607 people on its permanent payroll.

Just 10 years ago a typical manufacturing company's workforce was made up mostly of blue-collar workers. Today white-collar employees make up about 50 percent of a manufacturing company's workforce.

It was difficult for those in British Leyland: managers, staff or shopfloor workers, to accept change.

Mr Piech made it plain that management and workforce had to adopt a fundamental rethink if the group was to prosper.

Buick's robots either failed to deliver what was promised or they broke down. So, frequently, did relations between management and labour.

10 **Labour exercise.** Some of the words in the box go in front of 'labour'. Others go after. Find which go where and match the combinations to the definitions.

1 The willingness of people in the workforce to change jobs, or move to another part of the country to find work.
2 Organizations designed to protect the interests of workers in the United States. These organizations are known in Britain by another name. What is this name?
3 Workers with specialist knowledge and abilities.
4 A lack of workers in relation to the number required.
5 People who work with their hands.
6 Workers who don't cost much to employ.
7 Disagreements between labour and management, for example over pay.
8 These can be good, or they can be bad and lead to a lot of disagreements with management.

		shortage		
	cheap		manual	
mobility		**labour/labor**		relations
	skilled		unions	
		disputes		

Personnel or human resources?

personnel
human resources
HR
human resource management
HRM

The people working for an organization are, formally, its **personnel**. In large organizations, administration of people is done by the **personnel department**, although this expression is now sometimes rejected.

Companies talk instead about their **human resources** or **HR** and **human resource management** or **HRM**.

There has been some tendency for the term 'human resources' to be adopted as an alternative to 'personnel' simply for a change, or to move away from an image that has been associated with previous eras. It has also been adopted by some to avoid the word 'manpower', seen as sexist in phrases like 'manpower planning' and 'manpower administration'. Also, personnel managers seem constantly to suffer from paranoia about their lack of influence and are ready to snatch at anything, like a change in title, that might enhance their status.

11 Personnel criticism. Read this article by the authors of a report critical of personnel management and answer the questions.

HRM: BIG HAT BUT NO CATTLE?

Human resource management (HRM) has been the buzz-phrase in personnel in the past decade. All the management journals are awash with words such as 'commitment', 'employee involvement', 'profit sharing', and 'merit pay'. Unfortunately, virtually no HRM professionals, and few outsiders, have stood back and asked what all this activity has achieved. Our research shows that the description of personnel specialists as having 'big hat, no cattle': lots of pretensions but few results – is absolutely right.

Fortunately a survey covering over 2,000 workplaces has recently become available for analysis. This nationally representative survey – the Workplace Industrial Relations Survey – contains detailed information on companies using the new and the old style industrial relations. ...

Managers responsible for personnel matters were asked to rate management-employee relations on a seven-point scale, ranging from very good to very poor. Six different aspects of HRM were analysed – the role of the personnel manager, industrial relations procedures, payment systems, work flexibility, employee involvement and the status of the workforce. The results will be bitterly disappointing to HRM enthusiasts. Almost none of their techniques appear to improve management-employee relations.

Perhaps the most stunning findings concern the role of the personnel specialists and directors themselves. One-fifth of workplaces have a personnel specialist. Those workplaces have much worse relations between management and labour than those without. One objection to this finding is that the arrow of causation goes the other way: that workplaces with a poor climate might need the specialist personnel managers. We investigated this possible explanation but it was not supported by the evidence. ...

1 Are buzz-phrases and buzz-words fashionable?

2 Which job is normally associated with big hats and cattle?

3 If you have pretensions, do you promise more than you can deliver?

4 Industrial relations are the relations between em_ _ _ _ _ _ _s and em_ _ _ _ _ _ _s, in other words between m_ _ _ _ _ment and l_ _ _ _ _r.

5 Employee involvement probably refers to employee involvement in management decision-m_ _ing.

6 Stunning findings are
a) surprising, or
b) unsurprising.

7 Do the writers think that workplaces with bad personnel relations might have a personnel specialist because things need to be improved there?

Hiring and firing

'I have to be frank with you. Promotion prospects are terrible.'

'You're exactly the type of person I was looking for.'

recruit
recruitment

take (staff) on

hire
fire
hiring and firing

quit

Personnel departments are usually involved in finding new staff and **recruiting** them, **hiring** them, or **taking** them **on**, in a process of **recruitment**. Someone recruited is a **recruit**, or in American English only, a **hire**.

They are also involved when people are made to leave the organization, or **fired**.

These responsibilities are referred to, relatively informally, as **hiring and firing**.

If you leave a job voluntarily, you **quit**.

◆ **LANGUAGE NOTE**

In this context, **hire** and **quit** are used mainly in American English.

Everybody talks about the wonderful Japanese school system, yet every single Japanese company starts out with the assumption that the new hire has learnt nothing at school.

If the recruiter does not know the conditions existing in the department for which he or she is recruiting, how can the right person be hired for the right job?

When I started the course three years ago there were warnings of shortages of recruits in various professions, but I've written to a lot of companies and they say they're not taking people on.

No chairman of ICI, Shell or Unilever has ever been fired.

The European directive would require multinationals with over 1,000 employees to set up a council which would have to be consulted on, say, the company's financial health and its plans for hiring and firing.

12 Personnel problems. Is this extract written in American English or British English? What three features tell you this?

GOOD ENOUGH HATS, NOT ENOUGH CATTLE

... The personnel department found itself scrambling to meet the staffing demands of the plant supervisors. One consequence of this scramble for new hires was that selection standards were loosened. An increasing number of young, single and highly mobile workers was hired, many of whom quit after only a few months in the plant. The result: Personnel had to find replacements for people just hired as replacements.

Any organization having stable production levels plans a stable workforce level – that is, employee recruitment results in a flow of new hires that matches the flow of employees expected to terminate.

Unfortunately the lead-time needed for recruitment of certain trade skills was at least two weeks for local hires and as long as 3 months for workers relocating from distant areas. But Personnel was expected to find and hire replacements in less than two weeks. This became a major factor in the worsening relations between the operating departments and Personnel. ...

Delayering and downsizing

middle manager
front-line manager
line manager

Middle managers are those in the hierarchy between senior management and **front-line managers** or **line managers**, the people managing employees.

McGregor was called in to advise the CEO of a company who wished to ensure that his vice-presidents and middle managers paid more attention to employee development.

He is the person employees see every day. The front-line manager is the most important two-way communicator in any business. He is not only the mouthpiece by which company messages are communicated downwards, but the means by which messages are communicated upwards.

Top management looks to the HR department, as it does to line managers, to control costs.

'Who put a middle management chair at my top executive's desk?'

re-engineering
delayering
downsizing
rightsizing

lean
flat

Middle managers are now most often mentioned in the context of **re-engineering, delayering, downsizing**, or **rightsizing**: all these expressions describe the recent trend for companies to reduce the numbers of people they employ, often by getting rid of layers of managers from the middle of the hierarchy.

re-engineering 75 ⇓

An organization that has undergone this process is **lean** and its hierarchy **flat**.

lean production 74 ⇓

◆ **LANGUAGE NOTE**

Downsizing and **delayering** are also spelled with a hyphen.

To compete harder, companies are being forced to cut costs. Companies are sweeping away layers of management. (Texaco, an American oil company, has trimmed 11 layers to five.) This means that most companies will need fewer, brighter executives, not hoards of mediocre middle managers.

Whether it's called 're-engineering', 'downsizing' or 'delayering', the goals are the same: to eliminate tiers of middle managers in order to delegate responsibility to those actually running factories, designing products or dealing with customers.

Louis Gerstner, the new head of IBM, told aggrieved shareholders he would do everything to restore the computer giant to health. More staff cuts ('right-sizing') were needed, he said, strategic priorities must be defined and commitment to customers must be redoubled.

Wedekind was also told to bring in some lean management, a nice expression for the tough task of cutting staff from 156 to 92.

A flat organisation, with a small number of management levels, should give more opportunity for decision-making at all levels.

13 Corporate weight reduction. This article from *The Economist* uses the language of slimming to talk about downsizing. From the headline, introduction, and the article itself find:

a a word, used here in the plural, referring to an eating programme designed to help people lose weight.

b a two-word expression meaning a place where people go to lose weight and get fit.

c a formal word (a noun) referring to the state of being overweight.

d a word (used twice here) that means the process of losing weight.

e the comparative form of an adjective that can mean overweight, used here to talk about the amount of money that companies earn.

WHEN SLIMMING IS NOT ENOUGH

American managers are obsessed with corporate corpulence. But a downsized company is not always a dynamic one.

The gurus call it 'downsizing'. Last year, in an unending quest for lower costs, higher productivity and fatter profits, American firms announced 615,000 job cuts, an all-time record. In the first seven months of 1994, according to Challenger, Gray & Christmas, a Chicago consultancy, a further 319,000 workers suffered the same fate. Altogether, corporate America now spends $10 billion a year on restructuring.

profit *135* ⇓

restructuring *21* ⇑

The telecoms and computer industries, grappling with technical change and price wars, account for almost a third of this year's lay-offs. The remaining cuts were spread among industries as diverse as oil and aerospace, where deals such as this week's merger between Lockheed and Martin Marietta will lead to still more job losses. And yet, just when this most enduring of management fads seems to be permanently enshrined, American executives have begun to have their doubts.

merger *19* ⇑

It can make sense to cut back in stages. But some American firms have started to behave like corporate anorexics, addicted to downsizing as their only business strategy. A forthcoming study by the New York-based American Management Association found that two-thirds of firms cutting back in any given year do so again a year later. A quarter of the companies it studied had undergone three or more episodes of downsizing in the past five years.

Even the gurus have begun to wonder whether there is more to life than perpetual slimming. Gary Hamel and C K Prahalad, authors of a new book on business strategy, think that managers' obsession with downsizing can reflect a lack of imagination. It may be easier to increase returns on investment by cutting assets or jobs, rather than by raising profits.

Fans of downsizing disagree. They claim that in the 1980s entire industries – cars, defence, computers and others – needed a trip to the health farm, sometimes more than once. Downsizing is a way of freeing up capital and labour for growing sectors to absorb. What is more, there is plenty of evidence that downsizing has worked. American unit-labour costs fell by an average of 6.4% a year in 1985-93. In Japan and Germany, where downsizing has yet to begin in earnest, they rose at annual rates of 4.2% and 6.6% respectively. Recent business surveys show that America has become more competitive than Japan for the first time in a decade. Even if management fashion is changing, there is no case for most firms abandoning their diets.

sector *6* ⇑

Empowerment

empower
empowerment

Organizations say that they are eliminating middle levels of their hierarchies so as to **empower** ordinary workers and employees.

This process of **empowerment** is designed to give them the authority to make decisions that were previously taken by middle managers.

Empower your people. Don't command and control. Let them use their own initiative and entrepreneurial spirit.

...empowerment, an ugly transatlantic neologism which suggests that ordinary workers want, enjoy and benefit from being empowered. Of course, with power comes responsibility, and it is not clear that workers who warm to the former are equally happy about the latter. Also, the empowerment of one group usually means the disempowerment of another group, frequently the former's bosses.

14 **Radical empowerment.** Read this article from *The Economist* and answer the questions.

MANAGEMENT LESSONS FROM BRAZIL

Flattening corporate hierarchies, delegating authority and empowering workers may be today's managerial orthodoxy, but even the most caring of modern managers might feel

1 If something is orthodox, is it unusual?

that the way Ricardo Semler runs his company carries the doctrine of employee involvement to ridiculous extremes.

At Semco, a Brazilian manufacturer of pumps, mixers, valves and other industrial equipment, most employees decide their own salaries. Their bonuses, which are tied to the company's profits, are shared out as they choose. Everyone, including factory workers, sets his own working hours and groups of employees set their own productivity and sales targets.

There are no controls over travel or business expenses. There are no manuals or written procedures. Workers choose their own boss and then publicly evaluate his performance. All employees have unlimited access to the company's books and are trained to read balance sheets. Everyone knows what everyone else earns, and some workers earn more than their boss. Big corporate decisions, such as diversifications and acquisitions, are made by all employees.

Far from collapsing into chaos, Semco has survived, and sometimes even thrived, amid the turmoil of Brazil's hyperinflationary economy, which has obliterated thousands of other small manufacturers. Though hardly a roaring entrepreneurial success, this is no mean feat. Mr Semler expects Semco to earn about $3 million on sales of some $30 million this year.

The company has had to expand or shrink quickly to weather some rough periods, laying off workers occasionally and even coping with strikes. Today the firm is debt-free and has nearly 300 workers, with another 200 running their own 'satellite' businesses, set up as independent contractors with Semco's help. Semco's unique management style would be unique anywhere, but in Brazil, where authoritarian bossism remains in fashion, it looks even more bizarre. ...

Mr Semler's experiment in employee power seems to work largely because it is allied with some old-fashioned, hard-headedness. As owner of the firm, Mr Semler demands healthy dividends. And because a large proportion of the earnings of all employees is tied directly to the firm's profits, peer pressure on employees not to abuse their freedoms is enormous. 'It's really very simple,' says Mr Semler. 'All we're doing is treating people like adults.'

2 If you carry an idea to extremes, are you considered reasonable?

3 'Set' is used here as another word for 'd _ c _ d _'.

profit 135 ⇓

sales 114 ⇓

4 If you have unlimited access to something, can you see it whenever you want to?

balance sheet 134 ⇓

diversification 21 ⇑

acquisition 12 ⇑

5 If someone or something thrives, do they do well?

6 Other companies have been obliterated: they have gone b _ s _.

7 If something is no mean feat, is it easy to do?

8 If you weather a difficult period, you s u r _ _ _ _ _ it.

debt 128 ⇓

subcontractor 71 ⇓

9 If something is bizarre, it is o _ _.

10 Do hard-headed people have illusions about things?

dividend 162 ⇓

11 Are your peers people with the same status as you?

Getting the sack

'Better pull over and let me out – I just got laid off!'

dismiss
make people redundant
lay people off

lay-off
redundancy

When people lose their jobs, they are **dismissed** or **made redundant**. When people are **laid off** like this, commentators talk about the number of **dismissals** or **redundancies** involved.

There are many other ways of talking about this painful process, as the exercise indicates.

◆ **LANGUAGE NOTE**

The noun corresponding to **lay off** is **lay-off**, spelled as one word in American English.

Philips cuts: The Dutch electronics giant is to make 350 redundant out of a 1,200 strong workforce in Durham. Another 50 jobs in Lancashire will also go. Philips recently announced plans to cut 45,000 jobs worldwide.

Computer cutbacks: Olivetti is to sack 4,000 at home and 3,000 abroad.

Virtually all of Miniscribe's top management has been dismissed, and layoffs have shrunk worldwide employment to 5,700 from a peak of 8,350 a year ago.

Turner's staff dismissals became known as the Halloween massacre.

Midland boss Brian Pearse said that a merger between his bank and Lloyds would 'result in massive redundancies'.

merger 19 ⇑

15 **Parade of euphemisms.** How many words or expressions meaning 'dismiss' are there in these two extracts from the *Financial Times*?

SOFTENING THE BLOW 1

The language of dismissal appears to have as many euphemisms as that of sex and death. Those unfortunate enough to find themselves on the street may often wonder if they have been let go, terminated, discharged, fired, sacked, axed, given the boot, pushed or chopped.

The euphemisms for executives are more gentle. They retire, leave by mutual consent, part company to spend more time with their family, pursue an alternative career or accept a fresh challenge.

One of the most subtly disguised dismissals appeared in the film *Philadelphia*, when the actor Tom Hanks, playing an Aids victim, was told by his bosses: 'We can't make the best use of your talents.' At least the words 'You're fired' have a certain ring to them.

SOFTENING THE BLOW 2

We all know about downsizing, rightsizing, rationalising and other euphemisms for firing people. Yet until last week I had not come across 'involuntary separation'. Nor had the 1,200 Du Pont employees who on Thursday were bounced into this process by their employer.

There is no acceptable way of telling people that they have been sacked, but companies nevertheless continue to search for the perfect, painless phrase. According to consultancy Drake Deam Morin, there are more than 50 clichés in common use among managers giving their workers the chop.

They talk of 'careers that have plateaued', of 'decruitment', 'deselection' and 'displacement'. They speak of 'exiting the organisation', of the 'opportunity to look elsewhere', of 'releasing people', of 'retrenchment', of employees being 'surplus to requirements'. They say: 'your future lies elsewhere' or 'we are re-engineering'.

Outplacement

outplacement	**Outplacement** is when a company helps people it is making redundant find new jobs in other organizations.

◆ **LANGUAGE NOTE**

Outplacement is also spelled with a hyphen.

A round of redundancies can trigger loss of morale. Does the employer get professional advice early on? Outplacement consultants, as redundancy experts are known, train managers on how to make people redundant.

Outplacement activities for lower-level workers can be handled by HR staff, but for terminated executives a consulting firm that specializes in outplacement may be a wise investment.

16 Finding the right job. Read this article from the *Financial Times* about an executive who has been 'terminated' and answer the questions.

PEER PRESSURE FOR JOBS

...Lord Strathalmond, out of a job at the RW Sturge Syndicate in Lloyd's, is undergoing an outplacement course tailored to executives at KPMG Career Consultancy Services.

He is better off than most. Financially, the wolf is still some way from the door. He has a network of old friends and contacts that should, in theory, be able to provide a safety net of sorts. But Strathalmond is reluctant to rely on the old school tie.

Now, at the age of 46, Strathalmond has found himself for the first time in his life standing back and taking a long hard look at his future. The experience, he admits, is not free from fear or worry. But he is far from downhearted. 'I have always believed that change is the best sort of challenge,' he says. The outplacement was included as an optional part of his severance package. It gives him the use of an office and secretary and access to training sessions and techniques aimed at improving his chances of finding employment.

As a qualified chartered accountant, Strathalmond should not find opportunities wanting, but he is concerned to find the right kind of job and has set himself a nine-month target to find a suitable position. What this may be is not yet clear but he says he is seeking a job that will best utilise his skills. 'I want something to which I can add value. I know that when it feels right I will be able to tell.'

1 Your peers are a) people with the same status as you, or b) members of the British House of Lords. Peer pressure is normally the pressure that people are under to behave like people similar to themselves. What is the play on words in the headline?

2 If something is tailored for someone it is designed specially for them. Which three-word expression, also originating in clothing, means something standard and ready-made?

3 If the wolf is at the door, are you well off?

4 If someone relies on their old school tie to find a job, what do they do?

5 If you are far from downhearted, are you uphearted?

6 If something is optional, it is not c o m p u l _ _ _ _ _ _ _ _ _ .

7 If you find opportunities wanting, are there a) a lot of opportunities, or b) not many opportunities?

Strathalmond's position demonstrates that unemployment is no longer the preserve of the unskilled or unqualified. He is, however, obtaining the kind of help with job search not normally provided for the laid-off production worker.

The executive programme at KPMG provides private offices and secretaries on a separate floor of the consultancy. The idea is to provide a more sophisticated outplacement service, partly to soothe the bruised pride of losing a top job, and partly in recognition that the shock of losing the trappings of position can often be as severe as that of losing the job itself.

Other job-seeking managers and staff work in an open plan office environment where all have access to telephones, a research department and various classes, such as programmes on telephone technique or negotiating skills. One obvious benefit of this arrangement is that all also have access to each other to share their experiences. ...

8 If something is the preserve of someone, are other people affected by it?

9 Do open plan offices have walls separating them?

Stress

stress
  under stress
stressed (out)

overwork
overworked

burned out
burnt out

The people left in an organisation after it has been downsized often have more to do.

Stress is a combination of tension and anxiety often caused by **overwork:** working too much. People say that they are **under stress**, **stressed**, or **stressed out** when they are **overworked.**

'I'm sorry, but the only way I can deal with stress is by passing it on to others.'

People who have been under so much stress that they are unlikely to recover enough to do their jobs properly again are described as **burned out**, or in British English only, **burnt out**.

Japan's labour office ruled yesterday that a supermarket attendant, aged 43, who died of a haemorrhage after working 360 days in a row, was not a victim of 'karoshi' or death from overwork.

The awareness campaign addresses employees who are facing redundancy, under stress, suffering associated problems, such as alcoholism, or are generally unhappy in their job.

An atomic scientist killed himself with cyanide because he was stressed over his work, an inquest heard yesterday.

Sick of work, stressed out and desperate for a break?

Some people are burned out at 25; I'm alive at 35. Age is a state of mind and I'm defying it as well as I can.

17 **The survivors of downsizing.** Read this article from the *Independent* and answer the questions.

OVERWORK: THE NINETIES' DISEASE

If overmanning was the disorder of the seventies, overloading is the order of today. Fewer managers carry bigger burdens. Many are cracking under the strain.

David Black realised something was wrong when he began to fear that if he travelled home from work by Underground, he might throw himself under a train. His thoughts had been revolving around the sea and mountains, not as havens of peace and tranquillity, but as suitable places to kill himself. He saw the Underground as an accessible method close at hand. He decided to walk home instead.

What had happened to bring Black, a senior academic at London University, to the brink of suicide? He is a happily married man with two grown-up daughters, a comfortable home and a well-paid job in a respected academic institution. He is the author of six books, 50 articles and 20 published reports. He had worked at the university without one day's sick leave in 20 years.

1 A burden is a l _ _ _ _.

2 If you crack under the strain, are you able to resist the strain?

3 If something is accessible, is it easy to reach or do?

4 If you are on the brink of something, you are very c _ _ _ _ e to doing it.

The reason lay in the metamorphosis of his job. Like thousands of others in the slimmed-down, super-efficient, highly productive world of the 1990s, Black was being asked to do the work of two or three members of staff for much the same money with no extra support and no special thanks – a phenomenon that he calls the 'intensification of work'.

It has been described elsewhere as the 2:3:2 formula – half the people are now doing three times the work for twice the pay. As far as workload goes, the formula is accurate in universities, but the pay component does not hold good for academics, whose salaries have remained tightly controlled.

But even where pay has kept up with workload, it is not clear the price is worth paying. ... Black's misery is being replicated across Britain in hospitals, schools and commercial companies. While many people despair of finding work at all, many professionals in the private and public sector simply cannot cope, and, like Black, are cracking up. ...

Days lost from stress-related illness have increased from 30 million a year in the 1980s to 230 million a year in the 1990s. Howard Kahn, a lecturer in organisational psychology at Heriot-Watt University, Edinburgh, predicts a 'stress explosion' over the next few years because many companies have shed too many staff.

'Heart attacks will increase. Already we are seeing more depression, anxiety, irritability and accidents in the workplace. People overwork because there is more competition for fewer promotions; because so many grades have disappeared, there are fewer positions. There is more aggression in the workplace and more violence.'...

5 Metamorphosis is complete c _ _ _ _ _ e .

6 Support at work might be from a s e c _ _ _ _ _ y .

7 If something does not hold good for a situation, does it apply to that situation?

8 If something is replicated, it is r e _ _ _ _ _ e d or c _ p _ _ d .

9 If you despair of doing something, do you think you will be able to do it?

10 Companies have shed staff: they have _ _ _ them _ _ .

11 People who work too much are o v e r _ _ _ _ _ e d .

Crossword

Across

3 Short for personnel management under a more modern name (3)
5 Workforce (9)
8 Another word for 'senior' as in 'senior managers' (3)
11 Giving people more responsibility (11)
12 May also be the chairman of the board (3)
13 When a company employs new people, it ____________ (8)
15 and 7 down. What a company does when it changes its ways of doing things (2-9)
16 This may come in a package when an executive leaves a company (9)
17 All the ways people, especially top people, can be paid (12)

Down

1 Short for Chief Operating Executive (3)
2 These are human and there to be used (9)
4 These scientists work in finance (6)
6 Someone who likes starting new companies (12)
7 See 15 across
9 'Get rid of people' sounds less painful when this word is used (8)
10 Employees are made ____________ when they are fired (9)
14 Mogul (6)

Research, development, and production

Innovation

invention innovation research and development R&D research laboratory not-invented-here syndrome NIH syndrome

Totally new products are **inventions. Innovations** also include new ideas and new developments, including those that are less spectacular than outright inventions.

Invention and **innovation** can also be used as uncount nouns to show approval of new ideas.

In companies, new products are developed and existing products improved through **research and development** or **R&D** carried out in **research laboratories**.

When there is resistance in an organization to ideas or inventions that come from elsewhere, people talk about the **not-invented-here**, or **NIH**, **syndrome**.

Innovation is more likely to come from the creation of new organizations than it is from the redesign of existing ones.

An innovation is first adopted by a select group of buyers, who then influence others by word-of-mouth to adopt the innovation.

Once hooked on light bulbs, wheels and fax machines, people can barely imagine life without them. Invention is the mother of necessity.

'Like the battery, an invention is required for the fuel cell to work in cars,' says William Powers, executive director of Ford's research laboratories.

The strength of Rolls is that after spending £2 billion on R&D in the last six years, its range of engines is wider than ever.

This is one of the strengths of the IBM culture. Where there is a good idea, the general attitude is, well, let's take it, copy it, and do better. Very different from the 'not-invented-here' syndrome of other more individualistic organizations.

1 **Welcome innovations?** Read this survey of consumer attitudes to new inventions from the *Wall Street Journal*. How many innovations are mentioned by name? Which products do you consider necessary and which do you think are 'frills': unnecessary luxuries?

LITTLE WISHES FORM THE BIG DREAM

Inventions of earlier decades - the television, the air conditioner, the dishwasher - brought the American home communications, comfort and automation. But the Wall Street Journal's 'American way of buying' consumer survey found that the inventions that Americans value most are those that give convenience and control: the microwave oven, the video-cassette recorder (VCR), the automatic coffee maker.

Respondents were given a list of 19 inventions that have become major consumer items in the past decade or so, asking them to rate each on a scale ranging from 'made life a lot better' to 'modern frill'. Three-quarters of correspondents say the microwave oven has made life a lot better. More than 40% say the same for the VCR. In terms of products that give the most enjoyment, the microwave oven emerges the clear favorite, with the VCR second. ...

Of course, one consumer's life-bettering invention is another's useless frill. While older Americans cherish their coffee makers and remote control devices, they aren't impressed with computers, fax machines, VCRs or telephone answering machines. ...

Some celebrated modern inventions fail to impress modern American consumers. Roughly half those questioned denounce the compact disk player and the Walkman-style stereo as modern frills. ...

consumer 79 ⇓

Backroom boys and techno-nerds

inventor
researcher
technologist

boffin
backroom boy
nerd
techno-nerd

Although some modern inventions have a clearly identifiable individual **inventor**, this word, rightly or wrongly, suggests lonely eccentric geniuses working on their own.

Inventions nowadays usually come from teams of anonymous **researchers** or, more grandly, **technologists**.

These people are known familiarly as **boffins** or **backroom boys** which are slightly old-fashioned terms, or, in modern parlance, **nerds** or **techno-nerds**. All these expressions are often used by people who don't like or know much about technology.

◆ **LANGUAGE NOTE**

Backroom boy is also spelled **back-room boy**.
Techno-nerd is also spelled as one word or as two words.
Some people may reject **boffin** and **backroom boy** as sexist: there are no female equivalents to these terms.

...Bill White, the inventor of chewing gum.

Computer researchers face a double uncertainty: not only are they unsure what the technology can do, they are also unsure about what people will want it to do.

Science is always on the move. Its preference is to find a question that nobody knew needed answering, answer it and then move on, leaving technologists to turn the answer into a machine, a drug or a computer program.

Boffins in America have found a new way to make newspaper edible.

Lewis first became involved with defence work during the war when he worked as a 'back room boy' at the Ministry of Supply.

If you thought the Internet was for techno-nerds, think again. Over the past 18 months a vast new array of information resources has been added to this global computer network that even a novice can navigate.

2 **What's in a name?** Complete this article from *The Economist* with the names listed.

a ampere
b kelvin
c hoover
d macintosh
e ohm
f sandwich

WHO STEALS MY NAME: NAMES AS WORDS

...Many trades use an inventor's name: Lewis, a kind of gun, or of sheep-shears; yapp, a sort of book-binding. The name typically becomes an adjective, then, ideally, (if not to the maker), the generic noun: a Maxim gun, a Ford, a hoover. Use that last word (or say levis) as here without a capital, and a trade mark agent will jump on you.

You will tell him that ____________ (1) had already gone the further step into use as a verb 70 years ago (and do not offer him Hooverise instead; that means economise, after the future president who in 1917-1919 was America's food administrator). Many such words die with the technology: the hansom is gone. So are the brougham and victoria (users, these, not makers). But take off your ____________ (2) and you can still be brought a ____________ (3), like the 18th century earl, who could thus go on gambling uninterrupted. ...

Science has honoured its heroes with names like ____________ (4), ____________ (5) and ____________ (6). ...

Patents and their infringement

patent
infringe a patent

royalty

licence
license

Inventors protect their inventions by **patenting** them. Others may be permitted to use ideas for which there is a **patent** if they pay a **royalty** or **royalties**. They are then said to use the invention under **licence**.

Someone using a patented idea without permission is said to **infringe a patent**.

◆ **LANGUAGE NOTE**

The noun corresponding to the verb **license** is also spelled **license** in American English, but is spelled **licence** in British English.

No matter how brilliant, an invention is not your own until it is patented.

Polaroid alleged it had suffered losses of nearly $4 billion when Kodak infringed patents over a decade.

Japanese pharmaceutical firms began life by learning how to make foreign drugs under licence.

Texas Instruments' defense electronics' quarter results included $28 million in royalty income from patent licenses.

results 162 ⇓

3 **Taking on a giant.** Put the sections of this article from the *Guardian* into a logical order. (The first section is a and the last is f.)

JUDGMENT IS MUSIC TO SONY'S EARS

a A German-born inventor lost his 12-year battle to prove that the best-selling Walkman infringed his patent yesterday when a court threw out his case against the Sony Corporation. Andreas Pavel, 47, who lives in Milan, claimed he dreamt up the personal stereo while on holiday in Switzerland.

b The diagram for Mr Pavel's British patent, entitled 'Stereophonic Reproduction System for Personal Wear', showed something that looked like a cross between a diving belt and an instrument of torture.

c Mr Pavel had travelled to Japan nine times to argue with Sony. Litigation began in the High Court in 1988 and transferred to the patents court in 1990. It is the longest running case of its kind.

d Judge Peter Ford had told the court Mr Pavel's device was an 'evolution', not an invention. The case pitted Mr Pavel's timid patent agent, Keith Beresford, making his first court appearance, against the huge corporation represented by Baker McKenzie, the world's biggest law firm.

e Sony maintained that its co-founder, Akio Morita, came up with the Walkman as a way of drowning out his children's noise. Yesterday the Wood Green patents court dismissed Mr Pavel's claim. There had been minor infringements of his patent, but the patent itself was not sound.

f If Mr Pavel had won he would have been entitled to a royalty on each Walkman sold in Britain and would have become an overnight millionaire. Instead, he faces a legal bill of up to £3.5 million, and risks losing the rights to his other patents if he cannot pay. He said he planned to appeal. 'The Walkman came out of the blue and it was a big surprise to the industry. I'm completely convinced that it was an invention.'

Hi-tech and low

technology
information technology
IT

high technology
hi-tech

leading-edge
state-of-the-art

low-tech

intermediate technology

As an uncount noun **technology** describes scientific knowledge applied for practical purposes in general. A **technology** is scientific knowledge applied in a particular area, such as computing: **information technology** or **IT**.

Of course, some technologies are more complex than others. Products, systems, or industries using advanced technologies are **high technology, high-tech**, or **hi-tech**. The most advanced products and systems are **leading-edge** or **state-of-the-art**.

Things at the other end of the scale are **low-tech** (not 'lo-tech').

Intermediate technology describes things in between, and, more specifically, projects in the Third World using techniques suited to local resources and conditions.

'If we can't cure you at least we'll awe you with modern medical technology.'

Technology has made the world much smaller.

The rise of information technology (IT) means that many of the lowliest shop-floor workers need to be able to operate a computer.

shopfloor 43 ⇑

Murdoch looked at the communications technology explosion and decided he wanted a large piece of it.

Despite its superiority in many high-technology industries, Japan lags far behind the US and Europe in aerospace.

In Taiwan, Singapore and Hong Kong, manufacturers are producing the latest hi-tech products more quickly and cheaply than their German counterparts, who have neglected innovation, sleepwalked through a 10-year boom and grown fat and lazy.

The music is largely dependent on leading-edge technology. 'When you're doing electric music, every new device that comes along that allows for the creation of a sound that hasn't existed before should be of interest to you,' says Zappa.

Equipped with a lightweight Honda V12 engine, the car includes state-of-the-art electronic features borrowed from modern aircraft.

Like other places, Utah has to turn to low-tech services to soak up its growing numbers of literate job-hunters. Salt Lake City has become the telemarketing capital of America for mail order firms and reservation services.

4 **Small is beautiful.** Re-arrange the sections of this book review from *The Economist* into a logical order. (The first section is a and the last is f.)

MASTERING THE MACHINE: POVERTY, AID AND TECHNOLOGY
by Ian Smillie, Intermediate Technology Publications

a Mr Smillie's book, is, in part, a history of the intermediate technologies group, founded by Ernst ('Small is Beautiful') Schumacher.

b Mr Smillie cites Canada's huge aid to Bangladesh railways, ludicrous in a country where almost every journey is made by foot, boat or cart.

c Mr Smillie describes the many ways in which conventional aid policies can go wrong. Sometimes the fault lies with the belligerence of third-world governments.

d Sometimes the fault lies with the donors, who insist on steering aid into investments that may delight government ministers in the recipient countries, but do nothing for the really poor.

e Sub-Saharan Africa, he points out spent $2.2 billion on arms imports in 1983, compared with $1.7 on health.

f Schumacher's message was that poor countries needed to acquire technologies that are small, simple, cheap and under human control.

Rustbelt and sunbelt

smokestack

rustbelt

sunset
sunrise

sunbelt

Smokestack industries are traditional, old-technology ones, such as coal and textiles, associated with smokestacks: factory chimneys.

Rustbelt areas of the industrialized world contain or contained a high concentration of smokestack industries.

Declining industries are also referred to as **sunset** industries. **Sunrise** industries are expanding industries with a future, such as computers and electronics.

The **Sunbelt** of the United States consists of southern and western states that are increasingly attracting newer industries. Similar areas in other countries are now also referred to as the sunbelt.

◆ **LANGUAGE NOTE**

Smokestack, rustbelt, and **sunbelt** can be spelled with a hyphen or as two words.

Investment in the film industry is climbing rapidly. It is a sunrise industry in this country.

New figures compiled by the Thailand Development Research Institute show that for the first time this year exports of high-tech or sunrise industries have outpaced those from low-tech or sunset industries.

'People think of the steel business as and old and mundane smokestack business,' says Mr Iverson. 'They're dead wrong.'

Scotland's rustbelt is scarred with the dereliction of dead industries.

Two broad national trends have been discernible in recent decades: strong growth in population and national output in the hot, less crowded southern and western parts of the country - the so-called Sunbelt - thanks partly to the invention of relatively cheap forms of air-conditioning. At the same time, population growth has slowed to a trickle in the traditional industrial heartland - the so-called Rustbelt - and this region has suffered a decline in manufacturing output, as companies have been lured by the cheaper production costs of the South and its hostility to organised labour.

5 Drawn to the Sunbelt. Read this article from the *Financial Times* and answer the questions.

LONE EAGLES NEST IN THE ROCKIES: CLEAN AIR, OPEN SPACES AND LOW COSTS ARE DRAWING US PROFESSIONALS WEST

... Many of the companies coming to the Rockies are small - the kind of business that is creating most new jobs in the US - and many of them are in high-technology areas such as computing and medicine. For example, Boise, the capital of Idaho, a state renowned for growing potatoes, had the greatest job growth of any US city last year (6 per cent) and high-technology employment there has expanded by more than 10 per cent a year for the past six years.

Companies are attracted by the region's cheap labour (the Rockies have among the lowest average wages in the US), and modest costs for utilities, workers' benefits, housing and office space. ...

Some companies also hope the quality of life in the Rockies - with its wide open spaces, fresh air, low crime rate and small town values - will help them attract and keep well-educated employees. ...

The influx of professional individuals - such as fund managers, lawyers, computer experts, management consultants and writers - stems from two main forces. First, a large pool of these freelances is being created as US corporations, struggling to stay competitive, spin off service functions to outsiders.

At the same time, modern communications - computer modems, fax

1 What are utilities and what are benefits? utilities 7 ⇑

2 Is it possible to have an influx of one or two people?

3 If a company spins off service functions, it s u b _ _ _ _ _ _ _ _ _ _ s them.

machines and satellite television - allow professionals to live where they choose, if it is within striking distance of a good airport.

Mr Philip Burgess, who heads the Center for the New West, a Denver-based think tank, calls the breed 'lone eagles' - mobile knowledge workers who live by their wits.

'We are in an era of a great shift in lifestyle preferences,' he argues. 'More and more Americans are leaving big cities to pursue a better quality of life.' This promises to revive small towns in attractive parts of the US, recently deemed to be dying as Americans moved to city suburbs. ...

4 If you are within striking distance of somewhere, are you within easy reach of it?

5 If you live by your wits, do you make a living
a) with your intelligence, or
b) by doing manual work?

6 If you deem something to be true, you c o n _ _ _ _ _ _ it to be true.

Producing the goods

product

plant
factory
works

make
manufacture
produce

manufacturing
production
mass production

maker
manufacturer
producer

Products are **made**, **manufactured**, or **produced** in **plants**. A plant may be referred to as a **factory** or a **works**, but these two expressions are used more for older industries like cars than for newer ones like computers.

The process of making things is **manufacturing** or **production**. Making large numbers of basically identical goods is **mass production**.

Makers, manufacturers, and **producers** are organizations that make products. However, **produce** as a noun usually refers to agricultural products.

Manufacturing is also used when talking about the sector of the economy that makes things.

sector 7 ⇑

'Our factories are all out of the country. All we produce here are very rich executives.'

Perkins Group, the UK-based diesel engine producer, has signed a technology transfer contract under which two of its engine families will enter production at Tianjin Engine Works in eastern China.

From the middle of next year, Müller yoghurt products will be manufactured at a £14 million plant in Shropshire.

It now costs GM's plant in Russelsheim in Germany $470 more to make a car identical to that produced by the firm's factory in Luton.

If I was good with my hands, I would get endless pleasure from making a craft product. But I don't take any pleasure from mass production.

... two games makers, a small steel-producer and manufacturer of parts for robots.

Farmers were paid little for their produce, while the firms charged consumers high prices.

The number of people employed in manufacturing in the UK fell from 7.1 million in 1979 to 4.6 million in 1991.

output

capacity
- full capacity
- overcapacity
- spare capacity
- excess capacity

shortage

The **output** of a factory or plant can refer to either the type or quantity of things it produces.

A plant's or firm's **capacity** is the maximum number of goods of each type that it can produce.

When there is **excess capacity** or **overcapacity**, there is more capacity available than needed, implying that this situation is not a good thing.

Spare capacity, on the other hand, is often a good thing, implying that production can easily be increased if necessary.

Shortages of goods happen when not enough are produced, perhaps because plants are already working at **full capacity**.

During a period of heavy losses in the 1980s, British Steel cut its workforce by two-thirds and transformed its cost base by bringing capacity in line with output.

General Motors has signaled that as many as five of its US and Canadian plants may not survive, as it struggles to trim excess vehicle production capacity. The overcapacity problem has intensified in recent years.

With our recent investment, we have spare capacity and have recruited new sales staff to get our message across.

The recession should have ended last summer, but it has carried on.
If it continues, we will not be able to maintain production at full capacity.

recession *178* ⇓

Ford's truck sales have been hurt by a continuing shortage of trucks with automatic transmissions.

6 **Production partners.** Find combinations in the box that mean:

1 the buildings and equipment available to make things.
2 the sequence of steps whereby things are made.
3 the place where these steps are carried out.
4 the period from the design of a product through to final production.
5 the amount of money available to make something.
6 the quantity of products intended to be made.
7 reductions in the number of things being made.

process
budget
cuts
target
production
line
cycle
facilities

Robotics

assembly line
production line

automation

robot
robotics

CAD/CAM

Products like cars are made on a **production line** or **assembly line**.

Robots have taken over many of the tasks previously carried out by workers, part of the process of **automation**.

The use of robots in manufacturing is **robotics**.

CAD/CAM stands for computer aided design/computer assisted manufacturing.

Many of Asimov's predictions, including assembly-line robotics, pocket computers and a space walk, became reality.

Peugeot says its workers now fix faults immediately, as the Japanese do, rather than leaving them to be sorted out at the end of the production line.

Just 30 years ago, more than half the workers in rich countries spent their time making things. Nowadays well under a fifth of them do, because technology in the guise of automation, computerised production facilities and robots, does most of the work.

Poynter developed computer-based systems that improved the use of the laser-cutting machine, beginning the involvement with CAD/CAM.

7 **Undisciplined robots.** Read this article from *The Economist* and answer the questions.

WHEN GM'S ROBOTS RAN AMOK

We examine the ambitious automation strategy pursued by General Motors in the 1980s. Ten years and $80 billion later, it has failed. What went wrong?

After all the problems their industry has been through, it takes a lot to make American car-workers go misty-eyed. But there were tears in October last year when workers gathered at the giant Hamtramck plant in Detroit. They were there for the presentation of the Malcolm Baldridge National Quality Award. Although it was the first time that a car-maker had won the award, that was not the only reason emotions ran high. Five years ago this was the most troubled car plant in America.

It was at Hamtramck that an extraordinary gamble by GM with new technology spectacularly backfired. The production lines ground to a halt for hours when technicians tried to debug the software. When they did work, the robots often began dismembering each other, smashing cars, spraying paint everywhere or even fitting the wrong equipment. Automatic guided vehicles, installed to move parts around the factory sometimes simply refused to move. What was meant to be a showcase plant turned into a nightmare. ...

...eventually it became apparent that the way workers were trained, managed and motivated, not high technology, was the real key to competitive car-making. It is these people issues that GM is, belatedly, now taking on board.

1 Can things run amok in an organized way?

2 If emotions run high, do people feel deeply about things?

3 If you gamble on something, you b_ _ _ on it.

4 If something grinds to a halt, is it intended that it should stop?

5 If you call something a showcase, does this indicate approval?

6 If you take an issue on board, do you understand it?

Suppliers or partners?

raw materials

component
part
widget

supplier
partner

Companies providing **raw materials** and **components** or **parts** to a manufacturer are its **suppliers**. In modern manufacturing, suppliers are increasingly viewed and referred to as **partners**.

Parts are sometimes referred to familiarly as **widgets**, especially when their purpose is not clear, or when manufacturing is being discussed in a general way and the exact name of the part is not important.

A shortage of raw materials and components is forcing many industries to close down.

Many British component suppliers produce half the volume of parts with the same number of employees as their Japanese counterparts.

Mr Welch wants General Electric to be an enterprise where suppliers and customers are partners.

customer 79 ⇓

Suppliers are no longer a simple source of widgets, but are helping to design their client's products.

vertical integration
outsourcing
subcontracting

subcontractor

in-house

Vertical integration is where a company carries out more than one of the stages of obtaining raw materials and making components, assembling products and distributing them. The expression is also applied to similar situations in service industries.

Outsourcing is **subcontracting**: using **subcontractors** to do manufacturing that was previously done **in-house** and, increasingly, to provide services that were previously performed in-house.

◆ **LANGUAGE NOTE**

Outsourcing, subcontracting, and **subcontractor** are also spelled with hyphens.

Mr Peledeau has already achieved vertical integration. Quebecor can put a weekly newspaper on almost any Quebec doorstep without using outside help, from chopping down the trees to making the newsprint to flinging it up on the porch.

Vertical integration now appears to be the name of the game in Britain's holiday industry. Some Airtours customers could find themselves buying an Airtours holiday through an Airtours travel agent, flying on an Airtours airline and then staying in an Airtours hotel.

Sticking to your 'core business' or your 'core competence' is in. Doing everything yourself is considered unwise. Outsourcing (subcontracting in English) is for wiser folk.

core business 21 ⇑

Outsourcing leads banks to discard in-house technological expertise just when banking is becoming an increasingly high-tech business.

8 Lost in translation. Complete this article from *The Economist* with the words listed. (a occurs seven times, b four times, c and d twice each, e and f once each) and answer the questions.

a outsourcing
b subcontractors
c in-house
d production
e suppliers
f subcontracted

MANUFACTURING AND THE PRICE OF OUTSOURCING

Farming out chunks of _____ (1) to _____ (2), known to business buffs as _____ (3), has proved one of the more enduring management fads of the past decade. By handing over more and more of their _____ (4) to outside specialists, the theory goes, firms can cut costs, rein in capital spending and focus on what they are good at. _____ (5) plainly works: after all, Japanese companies swear by it. ...

Unsurprisingly, western companies have been trying to catch up. But like so many management techniques that seem to work well in Japan, _____ (6) appears to have lost something in translation. According to one study of over 100 manufacturing firms in America, Japan and Europe, many western companies find that something unexpected happens when they start using extensive subcontracting. Far from falling, their costs actually increase. ...

A number of the firms surveyed found that, after several years' _____ (7), they started to lose their technological edge over their competitors; others believed they were 'losing control' of their process technology; others that their product quality was faltering.

1 If you describe a fashion as a fad, do you approve of it?

2 What sorts of things can be literally 'reined in'?

capital spending *163* ⇓

3 If you swear by something, do you think it's a good thing?

4 '...appears to have lost something in translation.' Does this mean that technical documentation has literally been badly translated from Japanese?

5 What word is often used in front of 'edge' to talk about the advantage of one company over another in the same business?

competitor *80* ⇓

What were they doing wrong? Part of the answer is that most western firms start using _____ (8) simply because they want to cut overheads - shorthand in most cases for cutting jobs. Exactly which bits of the manufacturing processes are _____ (9) out is decided by which will save the most on overheads, not by which makes the most long-term sense. That means a piecemeal approach to _____ (10), which results in patches of manufacturing overcapacity scattered at random throughout a firm's operations. Trying to consolidate and reorganise the mish-mash of operations that remain _____ (11) is where companies usually trip up.

Approached this way, _____ (12) has other snags. It often results in the use of large numbers of _____ (13), as each part of the company delegates work to favoured _____ (14). That is one reason why Europe's mass market car makers have failed to cut costs despite extensive _____ (15). Co-ordinating a gaggle of _____ (16) is often more time-consuming, and costly, than managing _____ (17) manufacture of the parts in question.

Worse, the piecemeal, random nature of much subcontracting means that a company can lose its grip, often without realising it, on some of its core manufacturing processes. By the time the firm realises what is going on, it may be too late to make up lost ground. ...

6 If X is shorthand for Y, is it a way of saying the same thing in a different way?

overheads 115 ⇓

7 If something is found at random, is there a pattern to it?

8 Is 'snag' another word for
a) difficulty, or
b) advantage?

9 A gaggle is a group, but can it be an orderly group?

10 If you describe a process as piecemeal, do you approve of it?

Just-in-time

stocks
inventories

work-in-progress

warehouse

delivery

just-in-time
JIT

lead-time

lean manufacturing
lean production

Components waiting to be assembled are **stocks**, or in American English, **inventories**. Companies may also have stocks or inventories of **work-in-progress** and finished products, of course. Stocks are often kept in **warehouses** before **delivery**.

stocks
149 ⇓

There is a tendency for manufacturers to reduce stocks, and hence the need to finance, store and handle them, by getting suppliers to make and deliver components **just-in-time**: just before they are actually needed. This shortens **lead-times**, the time it takes to make and deliver goods.

lean organization
48 ⇑

JIT delivery is an example of **lean manufacturing** or **lean production** techniques.

Some manufacturers in recent years have sought to control costs by keeping their inventories of materials low.

Södersten has given BREL a 12-point recovery plan. Central to the plan is a reduction of work-in-progress from £200 million to £60 million (17% of sales) by next March.

Just-in-time stock control (to free up cash to repay debt) improves manufacturing quality (because defects show up, and must be fixed, more quickly). That promotes both lower costs and shorter production lead-times.

With good management, American workers readily adopt the techniques of lean manufacturing, especially flexible teamwork and personal responsibility for quality control.

9 **Philosophy quiz.** The extracts discuss production 'philosophies' of recent years, some of which have been applied to areas other than manufacturing. Complete the extracts with the names of the philosophies listed. (Where there is more than one gap in an extract, the same term is used in each gap.)

a kanban c kaizen b benchmarking d total quality management (TQM)

1 Since Toyota had not got the money to stockpile parts and materials, Mr Ohno evolved the ____________ system by which the products are pulled through the system by market demand, rather than being driven by the supply of raw materials. Parts are made only as they are needed, and supplied to the next production stage literally just in time. The system is controlled by a series of ____________, the word for 'sign' in Japanese. These are metal tickets or cards which act as an order from a workstation to the one before it, saying make X number of Y parts.

2 The Post Office sent two senior managers to the US to study the collection of management techniques and philosophy now called ____________. What they found was an influential circle of companies devoted to the principle that doing a job right first time is always cheaper in the long term than doing it approximately and fixing mistakes afterwards, as most firms do. In the fully-fledged ____________ organisation, quality is 'free'.

3 A central tenet of ____________, the Japanese concept of continuous improvement, is the elimination of waste. It not only exists in obvious piles of excess inventory. It is also wasteful when an operator makes more movements than is necessary to complete a task because his or her machine is badly positioned. ... Another central theme is the drive to reduce the time wasted in processes that do not add value, like carrying parts or moving from one machine to another. Willats says that in an average factory only one second is spent adding value - like drilling holes, assembling or packing - for every 1,000 seconds spent not adding value. He says he has never seen a factory cut this ratio to less than 1:200 but that managers and workers should continuously seek ways to reduce time-wasting effort.

4 ____________ - the practice of comparing business practices between companies - has come of age in the UK. ... Some ____________ success stories are the stuff of management textbooks. Rover halved its test times after ____________ against Honda. Lucas Industries cut the number of shopfloor grades four-fold following a ____________ exercise against a German plant. British Rail cut the time taken to clean a train to eight minutes after ____________ against British Airways.

Re-engineering

re-engineer

re-engineering

business process re-engineering
BPR

When a product is re-designed or a production process is organized more efficiently, it is **re-engineered.**

Like other production 'philosophies' the concept has been applied to businesses and parts of businesses other than manufacturing, and in this context is referred to as **business process re-engineering** or **BPR**.

re-engineering
48 ⇑

◆ **LANGUAGE NOTE**

Re-engineer and **re-engineering** are also spelled as one word, especially in American English.

Porsche maintains that some models have been so extensively re-engineered that they are, in effect, new cars.

First there was TQM, then JIT. Now comes BPR, the most ambitious business acronym of all. Having been all the rage in the United States for the past year or so, business process re-engineering, like total quality management and just-in-time scheduling, is coming to Europe.

10 **Fad backlash.** Read this article from *The Economist* and answer the questions.

TAKE A CLEAN SHEET OF PAPER

Behind the hype surrounding 'business process re-engineering' lurks an important message to companies.

It sounds like a parody of a management fad, no mean feat considering that many people view management fads themselves as parodies of rational thought. Instead of learning from past mistakes and triumphs, say the proponents of 'business process re-engineering', managers should forget everything they know about how their companies operate, and re-invent their businesses from scratch. The reward? Leaps in productivity and competitiveness.

Despite its ugly terminology and grandiose claims, re-engineering has been embraced publicly by scores of companies, including AT&T, Texas Instruments, Ford, Citicorp, Aetna Life and IBM. Many firms began 're-engineering' parts of their businesses before the term was first popularised by Michael Hammer, an American management consultant. Hundreds more are now planning to do the same ...

One of Mr Hammer's favourite examples is Ford's redesign of the procedures it uses to pay its thousands

1 If you describe something as hype, do you approve of it?

2 If something is no mean feat, is it easy to do?

3 If you do something from scratch, do you build on a basis that already exists?

4 A leap, for example in productivity, is a big i m p r _ _ _ _ _ _ _ _.

5 If you embrace something, do you support it fully?

of suppliers. This operation once employed 500 people shuffling purchase orders and invoices among themselves. Ford managers asked whether any of these bits of paper were necessary. Now 125 people do the same job faster. The clerk at the receiving dock, using a computer to reconcile deliveries with orders instantly, accepts goods on his own authority and issues payment. Most of the successful efforts cited by re-engineering advocates are such nuts-and-bolts examples. ...

There may be big rewards in eliminating a company's existing methods, but there are also big obstacles. Paradoxically, one of the biggest, says Thomas Davenport, a management consultant with Ernst & Young and one of the earliest advocates of re-engineering, is a company's existing computer system, which can be so complex that it is too expensive and too risky to scrap entirely. One American telephone company, he says, admits that its computer billing system is a disaster, producing errors on 70% of orders for new telephones. But the firm's managers cannot face the 'nightmare' of replacing its vast computer system and related software with something new and untested.

Mr Davenport worries that re-engineering is passing from a fad to a cliché. America's Chrysler, he points out, claims to have an incredible 150 re-engineering efforts going on at once. One of his clients boasted of a decision to provide employees with milk instead of cream in their coffee as 're-engineering'. 'At this level, the term loses all meaning,' complains Mr Davenport. The backlash begins.

6 Is paper-shuffling a useful activity?

invoice *122* ⇓

7 If you reconcile one piece of information with another, you check that they a g _ _ _.

8 If you scrap something, you get _ _ _ of it.

billing *122* ⇓

9 If there is a backlash to something,
a) it becomes even more popular, or
b) there is resistance to it, perhaps after a period of acceptance.

Crossword

Across

2 This edge shows superior technology (7)
5 Get something from outside that was previously done in-house (9)
6 Using someone else's invention without permission: patent ________ (12)
10 Industrial area with dying industries (8)
11 Redesigning products and processes from scratch (2-11)
12 Advanced technology is this, for short (2-4)
13 The most advanced technology is ________-of-the-art (5)
15 Technologist working behind the scenes? (8-3)
16 If you don't want to find yourself in a 6 across situation, get one of these in America (7)
17 Things a company does for itself happen in-________ (5)

Down

1 Get a supplier to do part of the work: ________-contract (3)
2 Minimalist manufacturing (4)
3 This happens to things on the production line (9)
4 American stocks (11)
6 Mid-level technology (12)
7 Doing it all yourself, from raw materials to finished product: vertical ________ (11)
8 Specialist areas of knowledge applied to industry (12)
9 View this company as a partner, if possible (8)
14 One secret of manufacturing success: just-in-________ (4)

Products, markets, and marketing

Customers, consumers, and clients

customer
consumer
client

customer base
client base

There are a number of ways to talk about people who buy things.

Customers are individuals or organizations who buy things from shops or other organizations.

Consumers are individuals who buy things, especially when considered as members of large groups of such people.

Clients are individuals or organizations who pay for services provided by a professional person or organization such as a lawyer or advertising agency.

A business may refer to its customers as its **customer base** or **client base**.

The customer is king. There is increased emphasis on the importance of the customer and meeting the customer's needs.

Consumers are buying less jam less often.

Midland Montagu still have private dining rooms to give corporate clients the full treatment.

corporate *2* ⇑

Analysts suggest that while Digital has a strong customer base for mini-computers, many of these users went to other companies when shopping for personal computers.

Sylcon had built a small but wealthy client base through the family connections of some of its directors.

1 Consumer combinations. Find combinations in the box that refer to:

1 things that people buy that last a long time, like refrigerators or televisions.
2 a period when consumers are spending a lot.
3 refusal by consumers to buy things from a country or company that they disapprove of.
4 the feeling that people have about economic prospects.
5 the amount consumers spend, often referred to when discussing the economy as a whole.
6 the study of how, why, where, and when people buy things.
7 the resistance of consumers to things or organizations that they disapprove of.

durables boycott behaviour backlash **consumer** confidence boom spending

Competition and key players

competitor
player
key player

compete

competitive
competitive advantage
competitive edge

competition

monopoly

Competitors are organizations selling products or services in the same market, and they can also be the products or services themselves.

Competitors **compete** with each other.

The related adjective is **competitive:** commentators talk about the things that give one company or product its **competitive advantage** or **competitive edge** over others.

Competitors in a market are **players**, and the most important ones are **key players**.

Competition is characterized in many ways: some of them are in the exercise.

Companies without competitors are **monopolies**.

'Wonderful news, J.B. Our competitors are losing money faster than we are.'

Like most businesses, British Airways would rather be rid of its competitors.

Despite the inevitable comparison with Compaq, however, Texas Instruments' new notebook won't be a direct competitor.

European airlines yesterday warned the European Commission that proposals governing airline reservation systems would hand a competitive advantage to American airlines.

In the words of one exporter, 'If you want the competitive edge, you've got to get over there frequently and let your foreign partners know you care about them.'

partner *71* ⇑

Fisons has suffered a setback in its ambitions to become a key player in the pharmaceuticals industry.

The merger of Nestlé and Perrier is a significant obstacle to the maintenance of effective competition in the French market.

merger *19* ⇑

Telecoms is still widely associated with 'natural' monopolies that competitive businessmen have to be kept away from in order to prevent chaos.

2 Competitive expressions Complete these adjectives used to describe competition. They all mean 'strong' or 'very strong'.

f_rm_d_bl_

_nt_ns_

f__rc_

s_gn_f_c_nt

competition

c_t-thr__t

t__gh

st_ff

Markets and market orientation

market

A **market** for a product is the people or organizations who buy it or may buy it, or an area where it is sold.

market-driven
market-led
market-oriented

Companies quick to respond to the needs of a market are **market-driven, market-led,** or **market-oriented**.

These terms show approval, especially when used by organizations about themselves.

Boeing has produced figures showing that there will be striking growth in the market for aircraft with 350 or more seats.

Japan has tried to block imports of various uncomfortably cheap foreign products, claiming unique conditions in the Japanese market. French skis, for example, were not allowed in because it was said that Japanese snow was different from Alpine snow and therefore they could not function.

Body Shop, to use modern management jargon, was 'market-driven', that is, it identified real demand, from real people, for something that those people were prepared to pay for.

demand 178 ⇓

If we can bring in the new Adidas and change it from being product-driven to market-led, I think we've got a good chance.

The argument is that organizations that are market-oriented, i.e. those that track and respond to customer needs and preferences, can better satisfy customers and hence perform at higher levels.

3 Market partners. Read the examples and complete the commentary.

...the long and difficult task of building a market economy from the wreckage of central planning.

From now on, factories that work without getting paid will go bust. Making that happen is the single most important step the government can take to push Ukraine into a real market economy.

It is sometimes argued that corruption oils the wheels of a hugely over-regulated economy such as India's, which would otherwise grind to a halt. There is something in this. A black market price, is, after all a market price.

Daniel Ward, director of consumer affairs for Nissan Europe said, 'It is a difficult marketplace for everyone. We do not see any great signs of growth in the last part of the year and it will be a slow struggle upwards.'

The newspaper made much of the fact that the Asterix Park did not sell hamburgers. Mr de Schonen said market research showed that customers preferred not to sit down for meals.

market economy
market price
market forces
market place
market research

A ______ ______ is one where things are bought and sold freely and not under government control. In a market economy, prices are decided by ______ ______, the factors that influence the demand for things, their availability, and consequently their price. ______ ______ is used to indicate that a price has been 'decided' by the market, and not in some other way, for example by the government. ______ ______ means the same as market. ______ ______ is the gathering of information on markets, products and consumers: on what people need, want, and buy; how and when they buy; and why they buy one thing rather than another.

◆ **LANGUAGE NOTE**

Market place is also spelled with a hyphen and as one word.

Slicing up the market

market growth
market leader
market sector
market segment
market segmentation
market share

segment a market

A **market sector** or **segment** is a part of a larger market, for example the market for trucks seen as part of the overall market for vehicles. **Segment** is also used to refer to a particular category of customers.

When companies try to identify or appeal to these specific groups of customers, they talk about **segmenting a market** in a process of **segmentation.**

Market share is the proportion of sales that a company or a product has in a particular market. The **market leader** is the company or product with the biggest share.

Market growth is the rate at which the overall market is growing (or not, as the case may be).

'XI: Buy low; sell high. XII: Covet thy neighbour's market share ... .'

General Motor's full-sized trucks have helped the No. 1 auto maker raise its share of this lucrative market segment by one point to 38.9%.

One approach is to use the occasion for which the product is used. Air travel, for example, can be segmented as holiday, business, or visiting friends or relations. Another approach is to segment people by the major benefit they seek from a particular product.

Once children become teenagers, parental consumption of chocolate declines as their children's declines. Additional segmentation was based on tourism and exports.

The growth in this market sector will be fuelled by the many new entries into the 4x4 business, including the Vauxhall Frontera, the Jeep Wrangler and Cherokee.

sector 6 ⇑

As in so many other Japanese industries, the market leader at home, Toyota, is not the strongest exporter.

For all its other businesses, Gillette means one thing to consumers world-wide: shaving. Gillette dominates the business in the US, with a market share of about 64%.

For example, in situations of market growth, an organization might expect to achieve its own growth in the market place; this is clearly different from situations where markets are mature and where market growth has plateaued.

4 Abbreviated segments. YUPPIES, Young Upwardly-mobile Professional People, emerged in the 1980s as a high-spending segment of particular interest to marketing people. Marketeers might consider the following groups as segments. What do the terms mean? Find the missing word in each case. Clues are given in brackets.

1 DINKS: Double ____________ No Kids.
(These couples have no children and therefore a lot of money to spend on themselves, as they both go out to work.)

2 FEMS: First-time Expectant ____________.
(These women may soon no longer be part of a DINKS couple.)

3 DUMPS: Downwardly-____________ Professionals.
(Out-of-work professionals fallen on hard times.)

4 GUPPIES: Green ____________-mobile Professionals.
(Environmentally aware, but ambitious in their careers.)

5 BOBOS: Burnt-____________ But Opulent people.
(Rich, but exhausted.)

6 SWELLS: Single Women ____________ Lots in London.
(Unmarried women on high salaries in London.)

Products, goods, and services

product
good
goods
fast-moving consumer goods
FMCG
white goods
brown goods

A **product** is something that is produced or manufactured and sold, often in large numbers.

manufacture 67 ⇑

Products are sometimes referred to as **goods**, for example in the expression **fast-moving consumer goods**, or **FMCG**.

White goods are things such as washing machines and refrigerators. **Brown goods** are things such as televisions and hi-fi equipment.

However, it is unusual to talk about a **good**, except in specialized contexts such as economics or business studies.

'Before Vincent begins his presentation I would like to remind you that in our last get together we agreed that it was absolutely necessary to reposition your product for today's market.'

Gillette vastly under-estimated its product's potential.

...the whole process of transforming a good from its basic inputs into a final product.

Indonesia's manufactured goods now earn more abroad than its exports of oil and gas.

...the food, drinks, detergent and tobacco industries, indeed of all companies dealing in what marketers call fast-moving consumer goods.

Our poll shows significant rises in those who say they plan to buy a TV or video, though there is still little movement in the index for white goods such as fridges and freezers.

The popularity of home entertainment will be maintained over the period, with sales of brown goods such as televisions and hi-fi equipment, set to increase by 35 per cent, the report says.

merchandise

services

Goods are also referred to formally as **merchandise**.

Services are activities such as banking, tourism, or entertainment that contribute to the economy but which may not directly involve manufacturing. Services may be referred to informally as products, as in the final example.

At the Universal State Shop in Hanoi, there are young men who tell you how you can find better, cheaper merchandise in the private shops which pay them to stand there.

It is much harder to identify changes in quality in services, such as banking, than in a car.

Herbert von Karajan dominated the Salzburg Festival and brought it to new heights. Yet while the quality of the product remained high, something seemed to be lacking.

5 **Goods as services, and vice-versa.** This is an article from *The Economist* about the distinction, in the writer's view a false one, between manufacturing and services. 'Services' occurs seven times and 'manufacturing' occurs six times. Where do they occur?

________ MYTHS

Dividing their labour and specialising, people buy goods and ____________ from each other. Car workers eat hamburgers: hamburger flippers watch films; film producers buy cars. All depend on each other, for each provides the others with something they want.

None is the place where the buck starts, or stops. But their jobs are not equal. Some activities earn more than others, broadly because they add more value, create more wealth.

Once, it was true that the most value was added in ____________ . No longer. Some factories add lots of value, some little. Lots of value is added in ____________. Nor is there a relevant distinction between ____________ and ____________, but it has become much harder to distinguish it.

Any product: a car, a semi-conductor, a shirt, is a bundle of different processes, some of them ____________, some of them ____________. The way that bundle is tied together has changed.

The designer of the Morris Minor and the Mini, Alec Issigonis, provided a service. Yet statistically he was a manufacturer, since he was employed as a car maker. In the 1950s and 1960s firms tended to perform many of their own ____________. What if Issigonis had gone off to run his own car design and engineering firm? At a stroke, the proportion of Britain's GDP in ____________ would have fallen and that in ____________ would have risen.

That trend, of contracting ____________ out rather than performing them in-house, was common everywhere in the 1980s. It is one big reason why ____________'s share fell. ...

Product scenarios

introduce a product launch a product recall a product withdraw a product product introduction launch recall withdrawal

New products are **introduced** or **launched** onto the market.

If a defect is found in a product after it is launched, it may be **recalled**: customers may be asked to return the defective product for checks.

A product that a company no longer wants to make available is **withdrawn** from the market.

The equivalent nouns are shown on the left.

He plans to test Prize Frize for a year in southern California and then to launch the product nationally.

Dell has made its biggest product launch so far, with 18 new PCs to replace its current line.

Rumors about the new product introductions have been pushing Compaq stock prices higher.

stock 149 ⇓

Coping with the recall of a defective product (eg defective brakes on cars) is an example of a tactical planning problem.

If a drug company receives complaints from doctors who have prescribed its product, should it then withdraw the product or warn other doctors of the problem?

The hypothesis is, that after the launch of a new product, its sales will tend to follow a pattern or cycle that features phases of introduction, growth, maturity and decline, resulting in death or withdrawal from the marketplace.

6 Innovative nightmares. This is an article from the *Financial Times* about new product launches. Complete the article with the numbered names. (One name is used twice.)

a OAW
b SPEW
c MENTADENT
d NEON SUCETTES
e HOT 'N' COLD

WAKEY WAKEY – OPEN YOUR EYES TO NEW PRODUCTS

__________ (1) is every parent's nightmare: the fruit-flavoured powder, available in the US, makes a coloured foam in the mouth, and is sold complete with a reflecting 'Spewer Viewer' so children can check the effect.

__________ (2) is a French canine 'sports drink' which is said to refresh and revive dogs after they have been exercising.

__________ (3) is a Danish bread-and-ice-cream sandwich which can be served grilled, fried or toasted.

Spew, Oaw, and Hot 'n' Cold are just three of the 12,000 new products which have been unleashed on unsuspecting consumers around the world in the past year, according to the market research group Mintel. Its 450 field researchers – who shop for the new, the bizarre and the handful of products which will still be on the shelves by next year – report that product innovation has been continuing unabated, even in those economies affected by recession.

Six product areas account for about a quarter of all launches listed last year by Mintel in its fortnightly new product reports: confectionery; desserts and ice creams; sauces and seasonings; soft drinks; haircare; and oral hygiene.

New launches in confectionery have ranged from the vitamin-enriched and sugar-free, to the high-calorie and luridly-coloured. In France, ___________ (4) are lollipops which stain the tongue 'electric blue', 'toad green', or 'Dracula red'. At the same time, France has also seen the launch of 'natural' fruit gums which claim to help keep the 'intestinal eco-system' in good order.

The Japanese appear to be keen on what Mintel terms 'functional' foods. For example, Wakey is a gum which wards off sleepiness, while ___________ (5) have extended their range to include apple mint for etiquette, herb mint for relaxation, and jasmine mint for elegance.

A new drink based on dokudami, a foul-smelling plant, 'helps quicken blood flow, promotes urination and prevents various adult diseases'. The wonder drink is also said to be 'efficacious against piles and constipation'.

In personal care products, the 'two-in-one' trend, which began with shampoos and conditioners, now seems to be working its way through bath and toothpaste new launches. ___________ (6) , for example, is being packaged in a dual-chambered container which dispenses baking powder and hydrogen peroxide solutions. Not unlike Spew or Neon Sucettes, the effect is blue and effervescent.

Mr David Jago, Mintel's new products specialist, says that most new product launches are doomed to failure. 'I'd hazard a guess that around 70-80 per cent of all product introductions don't succeed in the long term,' he says.

7 Product combinations. Find combinations in the box on the next page that mean:

1 the products that a company has to offer, considered as a group. (4 expressions)
2 the life of a product considered in terms of the phases from its development and launch to its withdrawal.
3 the way a product is designed to be perceived in relation to other products.
4 a company paying for its product to be used or seen in a film or tv programme.

'Product placement has gotten so obtrusive.'

		mix		
	lifecycle		range	
positioning		**product**		placement
	portfolio		line	

◆ **LANGUAGE NOTE**

Lifecycle is also spelled with a hyphen and as two words.

Now match the two parts of these extracts.

1 Boeing is now expanding its product line with its first all-new aircraft for 12 years.
2 Mitre's product range includes soccer
3 British Aerospace said more than half its sales now come from
4 By rearranging what each supplier can do on its network,
5 As product lifecycles shorten,
6 The entire multi-million dollar event has been designed to complement Pepsi Max's sporty
7 The Bond films were the first to realise the potential of product placement. 007 had more than a licence to kill.

supplier 71 ⥣

a the lifespan of some consumer electronics gadgets is now as short as six months.
b products that weren't included in its product portfolio as little as two years ago.
c Nike can change its product mix almost overnight.
d At present the company makes four models, the 737, 757, 767 and the $150 million 747.
e and rugby balls and sports footwear.
f The logo was a licence to print money, with spin-off merchandise ranging from James Bond pyjamas to eau-de-cologne.
g positioning as a low-calorie cola drink for youths wanting to 'live life to the Max'.

Cash cows and loss leaders

money spinner
cash cow
loss leader

A product or business generating a lot of profit is a **money spinner**.

Technically, a **cash cow** is a profitable product or business with high market share in a low-growth market, but it is also used to mean any profitable product or business generating a steady flow of sales revenues.

A **loss leader** is a product sold unprofitably in order to attract customers who will then, it is hoped, be persuaded to buy profitable ones.

Railcards are a commercial venture which improve British Rail's overall revenue position by creating an up-front revenue stream from the sale of cards and by generating additional journeys. But they are not significant money spinners.

Imperial is the classic Hanson cash-cow: a mature business, tied to British markets with low investment needs, retrenched by Hanson to a few lucrative brands pumping money to Hanson head office.

In Britain, where the trade promotion system is not as complicated as in America, supermarkets sometimes sell top brands below cost as loss leaders, thereby angering manufacturers.

8 **Loss leader package holidays.** This article about loss leader selling techniques is from *The Times*. Re-arrange the sections into a logical order. (The first paragraph is a and the last is e. Local authority trading standards officers (paragraph c) are government officials who make sure that shops and business trade fairly, without cheating consumers. 'Ruse' (paragraph e) means 'trick'.)

TRAVEL AGENTS WARNED OVER ADVERTS

a Many late-booking holiday makers are being wooed into travel agencies by cut-price offers then given a hard sell to encourage them to book more expensive packages.

b 'The problem is getting people through the doors. You can offer them a fortnight in Majorca for £69, then once they are inside, you point out all the drawbacks, such as that the hotels cannot be guaranteed, and sell them as many add-ons as possible.'

c Local authority trading standards officers have contacted ABTA after complaints that travel agents have left offers in windows long after all holidays have been sold. Travel agents have been told to ensure that their advertising is fair and accurate.

d Mike Grindrod, president of the Association of British Travel Agents (ABTA), said that to sell off thousands of unsold package holidays, travel agents were advertising loss leaders in their windows and then using trained staff to persuade holidaymakers to spend far more.

e The loss leaders, however, are still appearing in shop windows. At Thomas Cook in High Holborn, central London, a 14-night Athens package, including hotel accommodation, was being offered for £269. 'You won't know what hotel you're staying in until you arrive,' the assistant said. 'It may be better to look at Skiathos for £349 or Rhodes for £319.' The ruse is clearly working, as many tour operators report that most August holidays have been sold with little discounting. ...

Brand image

brand brand label brand name brand awareness brand recognition own-brand product own-label product generic product generics

A **brand** of a product is a version of it made by one particular manufacturer.

Consumers may or may not recognize or know about a particular **brand name** or **brand label**. This knowledge, or lack or it, is measured in terms of **brand recognition** and **brand awareness**.

A product sold by a retailer under the retailer's name rather than the manufacturer's is an **own-brand product** or **own-label product**.

Products that are not **branded**, not sold under a brand name, are **generic products**, or **generics**. This applies especially to pharmaceutical drugs.

◆ **LANGUAGE NOTE**

Brand name is also spelled with a hyphen and as one word.

Coke's well-known brand name would make the cost of taking it over prohibitive, analysts said. With the wide recognition of the Coke brand label, comparisons with traditional multiples of cashflow and earnings are meaningless.

takeover 12 ⇑
cash flow 124 ⇓
earnings 162 ⇓

Marketing programs are designed to enhance brand awareness and establish favorable, strong, and unique brand associations in memory so that consumers purchase the product or service.

Lever Brothers also advertises the micro system for two of their other brands, Radion and Surf, and then there are the many own-brand products of major supermarkets.

I should point out that Tesco's own-label South African chardonnay is really rather tasty.

Health authorities all round the world are trying to cut drug costs by using generic products and restricting price increases on branded drugs.

...a loss of public confidence in so-called generics – low-cost copies of brandname drugs whose patents have expired.

patent 62 ⇑

image brand image Marlboro Friday

The perception that people have of a person, product, service, or organization is their **image**, and the perception they have of a brand is its **brand image**.

A key event in the recent history of brands was **Marlboro Friday**: see the example.

Plummer (1985) asserts that one component of brand image is the personality of character of the brand itself. He summarizes research demonstrating that brands can be characterized by personality descriptors such as 'youthful', 'colorful' and 'gentle'.

Larry Light, a marketing guru, says that 'brands are being bargained, belittled, bartered and battered'. Will 1993 be remembered as the year the spell was broken? If it is, the day that will live in infamy is 'Marlboro Friday'. This was April 2nd, when Philip Morris admitted that one of the world's most powerful and profitable brands was losing out to cheaper cigarettes most people had never heard of. As it slashed Marlboro's price, Wall Street wailed. In one day, investors not only wiped $13.4 billion off Philip Morris's stock market value, but also dumped shares in scores of other consumer-goods firms. RJR, Procter and Gamble, Coca-Cola, PepsiCo, Quaker Oats were all bludgeoned by traders convinced that the explosive growth once delivered by branded standard-bearers was a thing of the past.

9 **Brand dilution?** Read this article from the *Independent on Sunday* and answer the questions.

STRETCHING A BRAND TO THE BREAK POINT

Both Marks and Spencer, by selling underwear and pensions, and Virgin, with flights to New York and cans of cola, have seized opportunities for extending their brand names into new areas. But it is difficult to manage successfully. If you stretch a brand too far, the elastic can snap and the core value of the name becomes devalued, as some companies have found to their cost.

Brand extension has become valuable in the past five years. During the recession, hard-pressed marketing directors in the food industry offered consumers more choice by adding new flavours, taking out fat or sugar, or moving from one tried and tested category, such as confectionery, to an allied one such as soft drinks. It was a low-risk strategy – it avoided the huge costs of new product development and offered variation on an existing purchase.

A new flavour or a move to an allied area, such as Persil washing-up liquid or Mars ice-cream is technically not too difficult to

1 Brands have limited elasticity, and the elastic can snap or b _ _ _ k.
2 Is the core value of a product its central, most important characteristic?
3 Are hard-pressed people in a good situation?

recession 178 ⇓

4 If X is allied to Y, is it related to it?
5 Confectionery is chocolate and sweets, or c _ _ _ y in American English.
6 What are Persil and Mars normally associated with?

achieve, and does not require a leap of understanding by consumers who already recognise a brand's inherent qualities.

But some companies have expanded into new and unexpected areas. Among them are tobacco companies, which – by moving into sectors such as luxury goods and clothing – keep their brand names in the mind of the public despite stringent regulations on advertising.

Dunhill was one of the first to recognise the power of its brand name, and has successfully built up a luxury goods empire. Marlboro and Camel are associated with clothing and even travel.

Laura Haynes, managing director of the branding specialist Beresfords, says: 'A company must identify what it is about the brand that makes it special – what are its core values? Can you move in a linear way? Cadbury, for example, could not use its name on frozen fish – it wouldn't work – but Porsche might be able to move into watches, because the name is synonymous with excellence and style.'...

Perhaps the brand that is currently being stretched the most is Virgin. Last year, Richard Branson told the UK's leading marketers that 'Virgin was more than a bearded brand in a sweater.' The company has subsequently launched a cola and a vodka. More products are believed to be in the pipeline.

But is Virgin pushing it too far? Probably not. The Virgin brand probably has more elasticity than most. If you accept that Virgin mirrors Branson, then he has a certain chutzpah, and that quality can be embodied in a number of products.

7 If something requires a leap of understanding, is it easy to understand?

8 Stringent regulations are strict ones. There are stringent regulations on the advertising of what?

9 Why wouldn't the name Cadbury work on frozen fish?

10 Why the reference to the sweater?
   a) Branson sells sweaters, or
   b) Branson is often photographed wearing a sweater.

11 Can only oil be 'in the pipeline'?

12 Is chutzpah normally considered a positive quality?

Pricing high and low

pricing

low-priced
mid-priced
high-priced

One of a company's concerns is, of course, deciding the price of its products in relation to each other and to competing products. This is known as **pricing**.

A product may be seen as expensive or cheap, but 'expensive' may imply 'too expensive' and 'cheap' is often used to show disapproval of poor quality. A way of getting round this is to say that something is **high-priced** or **low-priced.**

Similarly, things may be **mid-priced**.

In formulating its pricing strategy for the Macintosh, Apple faced a classic management dilemma.

The introduction of the lower-priced Cadillac Cimaron model is thought to have led to declines in image and sales for the entire Cadillac division.

Invergordon Distillers has launched a new value-for-money brand of Scotch whisky. Cluny will retail at a price between own-label whiskies and mid-priced standard brands.

Oreal spends 4.9% of sales on R&D and has become good at transferring the benefits of research for its prestige brands, like Niosome, a high-priced cream based on liposome technology, to its middle-market but high-volume Plenitude brand.

R&D *59* ⇑
sales *114* ⇓

10 Price logic. Which expression from this section is missing from all of these extracts?

Many of those travelling have been tempted by	....	package tours, such as a return flight and three nights
All the crops that we grow today are similarly	....	, meaning that the income of an average-sized farm
York furrier. He contends that chasing consumers with	....	products will harm the industry in the long run by
labour, China produces large amounts of high-volume	....	garments and textiles. Many of the world' garment trade
branded product and associating their name with	....	pills. Nonetheless, Merck believes it can grab the lion's
sports cars are under development. Porsche plans a	....	model. BMW may make a sports car at the American
competition. In the US auto market, from luxury cars to	....	cars, foreign and domestic manufacturers compete head

The war for sales

list price
discount
discounting

price cuts
price wars

undercut

A product may have an 'official' **list price**, but this price may in practice rarely be charged because of **discounting** by sellers who offer a lower price by giving a **discount.**

When prices are reduced, there are **price cuts.** When a business sells a product at a lower price than its competitors, it **undercuts** them.

Companies responding to each others' price cuts by repeatedly cutting prices engage in **price wars**.

◆ **LANGUAGE NOTE**

Undercut is also spelled with a hyphen.

The American Communist Party had sent Ho Chi Minh a wrist watch, a good 'Jules Jurgensen'. Back in America, I asked a jeweller about this brand. He said, 'It's the kind of thing you see in a catalogue. You know: $795 list price. Discount price $395. This week only $259.'

Average store sales this year were down nearly $3,200, reflecting a fierce discounting war among fast-food chains.

Kingfisher, B&Q's parent, does not like the expression 'price war', preferring to talk about a 'price initiative'. Kingfisher's chairman, Sir Geoff Mulcahy, says that the word 'war' suggests a beginning and an end. B&Q's price cuts are here to stay, he says: not a short-term promotion, they are part of a long-term strategy.

parent company 11 ⇑

British Midland launched a new business class on March 28th with fares that undercut its rivals' prices by as much as 40 per cent.

dumping

When a foreign company is believed to be selling products at less than what it costs to make them, or at less than the price it charges in its home market, it is accused of **dumping**.

The Commerce Department, upholding trade complaints filed by American Telephone and Telegraph, issued preliminary rulings that manufacturers of business telephone systems in Japan, Taiwan and South Korea are 'dumping' their products in the US. Dumping is selling in the US at prices below the cost of production or the homemarket prices.

11 **One country's export is another's dumping.** Re-arrange these sections from a *Financial Times* article into a logical order. (The first paragraph is a and the last is h.)

EU STEEL DUMPING CLAIM

a European Union steelmakers are to file an anti-dumping complaint,

b raising their share in Germany from an average 5 per cent in the first nine months of 1993 to more than 18 per cent in the final quarter.

c and had captured 27 per cent of total German sales by the final quarter, the Dusseldorf-based federal steel association said yesterday.

d Czech suppliers had been particularly aggressive, it added,

e alleging Czech and Hungarian structural steel suppliers have under-cut EU prices by up to 50 per cent.

f The complaint regarding structural steel, widely used in construction,

g The east Europeans increased their EU market share almost threefold to 9 per cent last year,

h will be posted later this week by the EU's Eurofer industry group, which will claim unfair tactics are costing western steel companies DM320 million (£130 million) a year.

Upmarket, downmarket, and mass market

upmarket
mid-market
downmarket
move upmarket
go upmarket
move downmarket
go downmarket

mass market

trade up
trade down

Products that are expensive compared to others of the same type are described as **upmarket**. Mid-priced products are described as **mid-market**. Low-priced products may be referred to as **downmarket**, but this term usually shows disapproval.

Upmarket and **downmarket** are also used as adverbs in expressions like **move upmarket** and **go downmarket**.

Mass market does not necessarily indicate disapproval and is used to talk about non-luxury goods that sell in large quantities.

If you replace a less expensive product with a more expensive one, you **trade up** or **upgrade**, and if you do the opposite, you **trade down** or **downgrade**.

'Perhaps we should go up-market and make it a "glossy".'

◆ **LANGUAGE NOTE**

Upmarket and **downmarket** are also spelled with hyphens.

We visited the showrooms of both the upmarket franchises selling BMWs and Mercedes and the mid-market fleet range selling Fords, Rovers and Vauxhalls.

As income increases, consumers demand better services. That tends to mean more labour-intensive and hence more expensive services, eg a move upmarket from McDonald's to the Ritz.

Gerald Kaufman wrote in 'The Times' that Radio 3 was 'plunging downmarket' and would 'degenerate into junk radio'.

The consumer slump remains bad news for brands like Nivea. In the last recession, people traded down from more expensive toiletries to mass market brands like Nivea. But that doesn't seem to be happening this time around.

Drivers trading up from the Fiesta will feel at home in the new Escort.

Philips and other companies hope CD owners will upgrade to a new type of player that plays music CDs and multimedia discs.

Business travellers can trade down to cheaper fares. In America, 80% of travellers, and in Europe 64%, now use economy or discount fares.

The Association of British Insurers are playing down reports of motorists downgrading their insurance policies.

12 **Market logic.** Match the two parts of these extracts. Which expression from this section is missing from all of them?

1	...a move that could transform the mobile phone from a businessman's tool into a	a	cosmetics are sold. Only one third of Noxell's products now come from drugstore sales.
2	That will be especially helpful in building Noxell's presence in drugstores, where about 55% of	b	item. The earliest machines in Britain appeared at the turn of the century.
3	With Video for Windows, Microsoft is bringing the capability to the	c	niche eaten away by specialty hotel chains that catered to the elderly, the wealthy and business travellers.
4	It took only 25 years for the vacuum cleaner to evolve into a	d	of Windows users. Like Apple's Quicktime, this is proper digitised video.
5	Its big green sign became a national symbol of a reliable night's stay. But in recent years, the chain has seen its	e	product. Gerry Whent, Vodafone's chief executive will announce that the company is creating a second brand.

From high-end to low-end

range line	The cheapest **model** of a company's product **range** or **line**, for example of cars or computers, may be an **entry-level** product: one designed for people buying for the first time.
model entry-level	The cheapest models in a range or market are also described as **bottom-end** or **low-end**.
bottom-end low-end mid-range top-end high-end	Mid-priced products are **mid-range**. The most expensive products are **top-end** or **high-end**.
niche	A **niche** is a specific area of a market which has its own special customers and requirements.
cannibalize	When buyers of product A in a company's range buy product B instead, product B is said to **cannibalize** product A.

◆ **LANGUAGE NOTE**

All the expressions spelled with hyphens in this section are also spelled as two words.
Cannibalize is also spelled **cannibalise**.

Although Bell's and Johnnie Walker have an increasing market, others have dropped back. The brand building has to be undertaken across our complete product range.

Airbus patiently develops advanced products targeted at holes in Boeing's product line.

He said current expectations are for an entry-level machine to be shipped in December, with all of the more sophisticated versions to be out by June.

ship 122 ⇑

Since IKEA's UK launch, it has steadily taken market share from Habitat. However, Habitat says realignment over the past two years as a middle to top-end retailer compared with IKEA's middle to low-end proposition has removed some of the threat.

The price cut reflects Apple's desire to boost sales of its lower-priced computers, which have been lagging behind sales of its high-end models.

A week in a mid-range hotel in the Alps can cost as little as £175.

The brightly colored new products looked more like toys than the adult models. Sony found a new market niche, but Mr Kaye figured that its prices left plenty of room for a low-price competitor.

Mr Smale changed the brand management system to a broader category management plan, so individual Procter and Gamble products no longer compete against one another. Now, instead of Spic and Span battling Top Job in the market, a P&G manager may oversee both brands, and coordinate advertising and sales to minimize the products' cannibalizing each other.

13 Competing with yourself? Complete this article from *The Economist* with the words listed. One of the words is used three times, the rest once each.

a consumer	c cannibalising	e image	g ads
b consumers	d cannibalisation	f sales	h share

CANNIBALISING UP OR DOWN?

...Even before Sensor reached the shops, Gillette and its agencies had stirred up uncommon interest in something that men think about for two minutes a day. 'Teaser' ______________ (1) appeared during America's Superbowl and all TV channels at once in each European market. ...

At $3.75, the razors were cheaper than many non-disposables, so few ______________ (2) would be put off, but expensive enough, compared with disposables, to maintain a prestige ______________ (3). Big profits would come from the blades: at 75 cents each, they commanded a gross margin of nearly 90%.

Sensor blades and razors accounted for $200 million of Gillette's $1.6 billion shaving ______________ (4) in 1990. By year's end it was nearly profitable, a remarkable feat for any new ______________ (5) product. Of course, Sensor ate into the market shares of Gillette's other razors. 'When you have 65% of the market, ______________ (6) is inevitable,' says Mr Hoffman. 'The question is, are you ______________ (7) up or down?'

Of Sensor's 1990 ______________ (8), 64% came from former users of other non- disposable shavers (52% from Gillette, 11% from competitors), and 29% from disposables: half from each. More encouraging, ______________ (9) of disposables in Europe and America were flat. That trend continued in 1991, as Sensor's ______________ (10) of the blade market doubled, to around 15%, in both places.

The lite version

There is a trend for standard food and drink products also to be available in a **lite** or **light** version, containing, or perceived to contain, fewer calories.

'Fresh, lite, cholesterol-free, high in fibre' scream the labels on food packets. Without their own laboratories, consumers cannot know if the labels tell the truth.

14 Lite lies? Rearrange sections of this article from the *Wall Street Journal* into a logical order. (The first section is a and the last is f.)

SARA LEE RENAMES DESSERTS STATES DIDN'T TAKE LIGHTLY

a Sara Lee Corp agreed not to call its 200-calorie a slice, whipped cheesecake 'light' after objections were raised from calorie-counting attorneys general in nine states.

b A spokesman for the food and consumer products concern said the cheesecake and mousse desserts are now called 'French-style'. He insisted the decision was made 'unilaterally' and not because of pressure from the states of California, Iowa, Illinois, Massachusetts, Minnesota, Missouri, New York, Texas and Wisconsin.

concern 1 ⇑

c Several states have cited Sara Lee's use of the word 'light' as an example of mislabeling and misleading advertising, and had sought to get the company to drop the word or change the product.

d The desserts – which the company describes as 'airier, more whipped, taller' – are indeed lower in calories than Sara Lee's traditional cheesecake, which weighs in at 230 calories a slice. But not by enough.

e The spokesman said to qualify for the 'light' label, the products must have no more than two-thirds the calories of the traditional product, or about 154 calories in this case. Sara Lee said it agreed not to use the word 'light' on other products unless they meet that condition.

f Sara Lee said the word 'light' was meant to describe the texture of the cheesecakes, not the calorie count, but that it settled the matter to avoid weighty legal bills. The company said it will reimburse the nine states for legal costs.

Getting to the outlets

distribution
distribution channels
end-user
sales force
wholesaler
retailer
retail outlets
dealer
reseller

Distribution is concerned with getting a product to customers, or in some more technical contexts, its **end-users**.

By what **distribution channels** does the product reach customers? Is there a **sales force**? Is the product distributed through **distributors** or **wholesalers** before reaching the **retailers** or **retail outlets**?

In some businesses, wholesalers and/or retailers may be referred to as **dealers**. Retailers may be referred to as **resellers**.

◆ **LANGUAGE NOTE**

End-user is also spelled **end user**.

Mr Fleming said British Telecom and Mercury should be made to set up retailer companies to handle all their dealings with end-users.

Novell has also shaken up its distribution channels for the markets in which it is strongest: small and medium-sized firms. Because of its own hardware heritage, Novell's software is sold more in the way that hardware is, through independent resellers.

HarperCollins' sales force have instructions to visit bookshops at least once a week.

Japanese doctors not only prescribe drugs, they also dispense them. The doctors buy their drugs from wholesalers, who typically sell them at a discount to the official prices set by the Japanese government.

As manufacturers, distributors, resellers and retailers suffer, it is good news for consumers. There has never been a better time to buy a personal computer.

One of the principal reasons behind Airtours' buying travel agencies is the increased opportunity it derives to use its own retail outlets to sell its own packages.

15 Forms of selling. Match each selling technique to its definition.

1 **door-to-door selling**

2 **franchising**

3 **inertia selling**

4 **mail order**

5 **network marketing** or **pyramid selling**

6 **telesales** or **telemarketing**

a In return for payment and a share of sales revenue, an organization licenses its (well-known) name to be used by food outlets, retailers, and others. Hamburgers, pizza, and clothing are often sold under this system.

b Famous for its foot-in-the-door approach, everything from encyclopaedias through vacuum cleaners to brushes used to be sold in this way. Now less common, as people are not at home during the day, or if they are, may not answer the doorbell.

c You choose things in a catalogue (or catalog in American English) and order by post, phone, or fax. Clothes have long been sold in this way (somehow they never look as good as in the catalogue), but now everything from computers to wine is.

d Participants buy goods (but not Egyptian artefacts) or services from a company and then sell them to the general public. They can also make money by recruiting new participants and providing training or other services. Tupperware, with its famous suburban tea-parties, were the pioneers in this field.

e People phone you at home or at work and try to sell you things. When there has been no previous contact, this is known as 'cold-calling'. Alternatively, you may phone an organization in order to buy something in a catalogue you have received from them. Anything from insurance to computer services may be sold in this way.

f Insurance cover against such things as sickness and unemployment, to cover loan repayments is sold using this technique: you have specifically to say that you do not want this insurance when filling in the loan application. Banks rely on customers not opting out in this way in order to sell the insurance.

16 The end of shopping as we know it? Rearrange the sections of this article from *The Economist* into a logical order. (The first paragraph is a.)

THE INTERACTIVE BAZAAR OPENS

a ...In both trials of multimedia technology, consumers will be able to use their television screens to browse through constantly updated 'catalogues' containing images and information about, say, shirts or vacuum cleaners; to place orders for goods by means of a remote control or mouse; and to get their chosen products delivered to their home.

b In the trials, consumers should be able to switch on a shopping service provided by CUC International, a small Connecticut company that looks set to be the leader of interactive retailing. ... Walter Forbes, CUC's chairman, claims that interactive retailing has three advantages over local shops.

c Mr Forbes's third claimed advantage is convenience. Survey evidence suggests that many consumers find shopping boring, and are increasingly reluctant to leave the house because of fear of crime. Interactivity means that shopping no longer needs to involve a wearying trip to the local mall or supermarket in the rain.

d The first two also underlie CUC's growth in non-interactive form: information and cost. CUC's 'Shoppers Advantage' service offers sales information about 250,000 products from hundreds of manufacturers. And since the retailer is eliminated from the transaction, CUC's members get discounts of up to 50% on shop prices.

e This embryonic industry is already posing questions over the future of every other part of America's $2.1 trillion retailing industry. Is there, some wonder, a future for department stores at all? Will the fast-growing mail-order catalogue business worth $70 billion a year, be submerged into interactivity? More immediately, should retailers fight against interactive shopping, or should they join it? ...

f Unlike existing home-shopping TV channels, these interactive trials will give the customers control over what image is on the screen. Ultimately, the customers should be able to create their own, personalised home shopping services.

Advertising direct and indirect

advertising
advertising campaign
advertising agency

billboard
hoarding

advertisement
advert
ad
run an advertisement

direct marketing
mailing
mail shot
junk mail

Advertising tells people about products, for example in newspapers, on television in **commercials**, or in the street on **hoardings** or **billboards**. Advertising is often designed and managed by **advertising agencies**.

An **advertising campaign** consists of a series of **advertisements, adverts**, or **ads** which are **run** in various media.

Another way of telling people about products is by **direct marketing**, using techniques like **mailings**, also known as **mail shots**: these are often referred to derisively by recipients as **junk mail**.

◆ **LANGUAGE NOTE**

Advert is used in British English only.
Hoarding is used mainly in British English and **billboard** in American English.
Mailshot is also spelled with a hyphen or as two words.

Today she has no voice box and has lost a third of a lung: one of a tragic series of former cigarette advertisement stars who have fallen victim to smoking-related diseases.

The agency lost a $15 million account for Nikon cameras when it mistakenly ran an advert for a new product before it had formally been introduced.

'Dublin: Rock Capital of the World,' proclaims a hoarding in O'Donnell Street.

Nigel Mansell, like his car, is a moving billboard.

The world's biggest advertising campaign rests on the denim-clad shoulders of that anonymous cowboy, the Marlboro Man.

In years past, no movie director with a shred of pride would think of dabbling in commercials. But directing TV ads has become downright fashionable even among Hollywood's biggest names.

The Direct Mail Information Service says the money spent on postage and production of the mail shot: an estimated £750 million probably generates around £7 billion worth of business. Through the nation's letter boxes last year dropped 2.1 billion items of what is usually referred to as 'junk mail'.

With the Citicorp system, a dog food manufacturer could eliminate direct mail promotions to the 50% of Americans who don't own pets. 'Direct marketing is a very expensive form if you're using it as mass advertising,' says Mr Howe.

17 **The end of TV advertising as we know it?** Complete this article from the *Financial Times* with the expressions listed. (a occurs four times, b four times, c and d once each, e three times and f twice.)

a direct marketing
b advertising
c campaign
d discounting
e brands
f branded

HEINZ DROPS TV ADVERTS IN MOVE TO DIRECT MARKETING

HJ HEINZ, the food manufacturer that brought the British public such memorable advertising campaigns as Beanz Meanz Heinz, is planning to create a new slogan – Heinz Meanz ____________ (1).

Mr Tony O'Reilly, the flamboyant chairman and chief executive of the Pittsburg-based international food group, is planning to end UK commercial television ____________ (2) for his products this year and instead concentrate on ____________ (3) .

Mr O'Reilly, whose career in marketing took off after he created the Kerrygold ____________ (4) for Irish butter in his early 20s, believes the era of mass marketing is giving way to more targeted selling techniques.

The Heinz plan to give up television ____________ (5) would be one of the most radical marketing moves in recent years by a food manufacturer. It comes as manufacturers of ____________ (6) food products are facing growing competition from cheaper, own-label goods produced by supermarkets. The Heinz account is one of the longest established in television ____________ (7) .

Heinz has already built up a database of 5.6 million homes in the UK that are heavy users of the company's products. Mr O'Reilly plans to send special discount vouchers directly to those homes, thereby bypassing conventional ____________ (8) media such as television and newspapers. The discount vouchers will be for individual Heinz products, such as baked beans, but also for groups of Heinz lines.

Mr O'Reilly has decided that ____________ (9) is the most cost effective way of maintaining loyalty to the ____________ (10) . The Heinz chief executive sees the plan as the start of a 'guerrilla' campaign against the increasing power of the large supermarket groups, which, he believes, sometimes treat ____________ (11) products cavalierly. Mr O'Reilly wants to take control of ____________ (12) policy for his ____________ (13) rather than leaving it to the discretion of supermarkets. He is concerned that Heinz products are often treated as mid-market products when they should be priced and displayed as premium ____________ (14) . If Heinz goes ahead with its plan and proves that ____________ (15) to its best customers works, it could be a blow to commercial television.

Promoting the product

promotion

offer
freebie

point-of-sale

merchandising

The **promotion** of a product may refer to any marketing effort to encourage people to buy it, including advertising.

However, promotion is often used to refer specifically to marketing activities other than advertising: **offers** such as discounts, cut-price vouchers, free gifts (known informally as **freebies**), competitions, and displays or events at the **point-of-sale**, the place in the retail outlet where the product is sold.

Discounts may be given in a **sale** at a particular time of year such as summer or January, often to get rid of remaining stock.

Merchandising refers to the ways goods are presented at the point of sale, and more commonly, to goods such as toys and T-shirts that are produced to promote things like films or rock groups.

Despite heavy promotion, new car sales rose by only 1.7% in August over the figure for August last year.

Heinz, which has run effective promotions offering a free car a day for 100 days, probably had good reasons for recently announcing a shift of spending from TV to targeted promotions. Yet Hoover's free flights offer which sounded too good to be true failed because of confusion over the small print and inept administration.

...some of the hot new products in specialty advertising, the branch of the ad business that makes all those pencils, key rings and other freebies that companies give away to engender good will and repeat sales. Though sometimes known as the matchbook medium, specialty advertising racked up $4.1 billion in sales last year.

Although the number of drug salesmen may decline, firms may still need a big marketing operation to handle the advertising and point-of-sale promotion necessary in retail outlets.

Although he's moved to the executive suite, he still feels the best merchandising ideas come from retailers. Storekeepers, for instance, told him to keep stand-up displays short so that shoplifters can't hide behind them.

The studio can count on an impressionable market of children – and their parents – to boost sales of video, books, toys and other merchandise associated with film. Disney took $267 million at the box office in the first four months after launching 'The Lion King' in the US, but that has been surpassed by the income from merchandising.

18 Promotions from hell. The descriptions below (listed i to v) of disastrous promotions are from the *Independent*. Match the headlines 1 to 5 to the promotions they relate to. (The descriptions have been modified in order to disguise key clues.)

1 SUCKERS
2 SPLAT!
3 CROSS WIRES
4 TOO-FAST FOOD
5 EGG ON FACE

a Cadbury's chocolate
b Hoover vacuum cleaners
c McDonald's hamburgers
d Mercury mobile phones
e Wild Turkey bourbon whiskey

i For the 1984 Olympic Games in Los Angeles, ______ issued customers with cards carrying the names of various events. If the US won a gold medal in the event, the customer won a prize. A games boycott by most of the Eastern bloc, however, meant that the US collected an unusually high tally of golds and ______ customers won an unusually high number of prizes.

ii Six planes took off and unloaded their cargo of live ______ over a US city to promote ______ bourbon whiskey. Hundreds were released before it was realised that ______ cannot fly.

iii To quote Leonard Hadley, chairman of ______ US parent company Maytag, the UK company's free flights offer was like 'a bad accident and you can't determine what was in the driver's mind.' ______ offered any customer who spent £100 on its products two free flights to Europe and the US. The promotion attracted more than double the anticipated applications, leading to the dismissal of three senior managers and a £19 million provision to cover the anticipated costs. The market in second-hand ______ is still recovering from over-supply.

iv In the bid to transform the ______ ______ from the strict preserve of irritating men in restaurants into a mainstream consumer good, operators went into promotional overdrive before Christmas last year. ______ promised that anyone buying its One-2-One ______ would be entitled to unlimited free ______ worldwide on Christmas Day. However, massive demand meant its ______ seized up and many callers were unable to get through. ______ reported that at least 20 people had spent more than 12 hours on the ______.

v ... In 1984, the company buried a dozen caskets in locations hinted at by a book of clues. Each casket contained a certificate that entitled the finder to a ______ ______ worth £10,000. More than 100,000 people set about excavating the countryside. ... The Rollright Stones in Oxfordshire had stood straight since before Christ's birth, but are now leaning because rain seeped under them before the gold-diggers' holes could be filled in. The promotion was halted after the then Environment Secretary Patrick Jenkin informed Sir Adrian ______ of the archaeological vandalism for which his company was indirectly responsible.

The complete package

package

packager

packaging

A **package** is a collection of related things sold as one product.

It is also possible to talk about the way that non-physical goods such as films or ideas are **packaged** or presented. **Packagers** are individuals and organizations responsible for this.

Likewise, **packaging** can refer to the containers that products are sold in, and also the way that they are presented.

In this context, the expression sometimes indicates disapproval, inferring that the things are packaged so as to appear more attractive or interesting than they really are, as in the last example.

The Sweet Art Division of the Kauffman Machine Shop, Kansas, is marketing a computerised cake decorator that can transfer a digitised photographic image to the cake. The Sweet Art Series 1000 package includes a PC and camera, a robotic arm equipped with brushes, and a cake stand that is raised and lowered under computer control.

Telephone and cable service companies are forging links with programme packagers, such as cable television networks, and with programme originators, such as Hollywood film studios.

The Body Shop may have simple packaging, but it uses image just as much as Dior does.

Unfortunately for Schieffelin, however, government regulations hold that vodka can't have any distinctive taste, color or odor, which means taste isn't much of a marketing tool. Image and packaging are everything, which helps explain why Schieffelin is spending two and half times more on its fancy vodka bottles than on its gin bottles.

19 **Is less more?** Read this article from the *Financial Times* and answer the questions.

BUSINESS AND THE ENVIRONMENT: LESS IS MORE – MANUFACTURERS ARE TRYING TO CUT THEIR USE OF PACKAGING MATERIALS

In the early 1980s, when Procter & Gamble first test-marketed a highly concentrated laundry product, few people would buy it. Shoppers were put off by what they perceived to be less fabric softener or

1 If you are put off by something, does it attract you?

washing liquid at a premium price. Few of them seemed to care very much that so-called 'ultra' products could slash the amount of packaging finding its way into landfills.

But it was hard to keep a good idea down. P&G and other big consumer products manufacturers are now profiting from a shift in consumer sentiment. By 1993, 'ultra' – or concentrated – products were capturing about 70 per cent of the laundry market, according to Green Market Alert, a trade newsletter.

'Consumers once believed more is more, now they think otherwise,' says Jacqueline Ottman, a New York environmental consultant.

Concentrates are perhaps the most conspicuous success in the campaign by US companies over the past decade to minimise the undesirable effects of their packaging, most often by cutting the amount of material that requires disposal.

'Source reduction' is the buzzword phrase used in the field to describe a movement that embraces package redesign, 'light-weighting', and greater use of refillable containers and concentrates. It overlaps with efforts to promote recycling, which slows down demand for virgin materials. ...

Over the past four years, P&G has cut its use of packaging materials overall by 24 per cent, including a 42 per cent reduction in paperboard. It has also lifted the level of recycled materials in its packaging to 37 per cent, from 23 per cent in 1989-90.

'There is now a critical mass of recycled materials available to meet our needs and those of our competitors,' says Scott Stewart, a spokesman for P&G. ...

2 If you keep a good idea down, do you
a) suppress it, or
b) keep it to use later?

3 If there is a shift in sentiment, there is a c_ _ _ _ _ _ in a_ _ _ _ _ _ _ _.

4 More what?

5 If a success is conspicuous is it visible?

6 If you dispose of something, you t_ _ _ _ _ it a_ _ _ _.

7 If X overlaps with Y, does it duplicate it?

8 Is a critical mass a good thing in this context?

Marketeers and the marketing mix

market

marketer
marketeer

marketing
marketing mix

The **marketing mix** is often summarized as the so-called four Ps: product, price, place, promotion; what to sell, to whom, where, and with what support.

People and organizations who **market** a product make decisions as to how, when, and to whom it is to be sold: for example on its design, price, and distribution. People and organizations making these decisions are **marketers** or **marketeers** and work in **marketing**.

Marketing, of course, is also a subject taught in business schools.

In different markets the four Ps have different relative degrees of importance. Consequently, firms use these functions in different ways, or they mix them differently to give a particular marketing mix for a particular market. Therefore, the issue of marketing strategy is to determine how the four Ps are to be utilized, or the relative degrees of reliance that are to be placed on each.

Heineken now bring over what in Holland is standard bottled lager, relabel it in luxury-suggesting colours and market it as Heineken export.

One of the first things that Hanson did when it bought Ever Ready, a battery maker, was to sell the research centre and put the remaining scientists nearer the marketeers.

Like Nike, Reebok is basically a marketer, not a maker, of sports shoes. Its products come from shoe manufacturers in Asia.

Japanese consumers delight in buying the latest shiny new models from their country's electronic giants. But thanks to cunning product development and marketing strategies, these purchases are destined never to be quite new enough and their owners quickly discard obsolete models and fork out for the latest ones. In 1990, Tokyoites threw out 128,000 televisions, 88,000 washing machines, 100,000 fridges and 190,000 bicycles.

giant 11 ⇑

20 The end of marketing as we know it?

Read the following article from *The Economist* and answer the questions.

DEATH OF THE BRAND MANAGER

Brands are still alive, but keeping them so may mean killing off the marketing department.

At the start of this year, Unilever's British soaps arm, Lever brothers, abolished the job of marketing director. A year earlier, Elida Gibbs, the Anglo-Dutch conglomerate's personal-products division had done the same.

Though the details vary slightly, both companies have squashed together what used to be called the 'marketing' and 'sales' departments, and then re-organised them as a series of 'business groups', focusing on consumer research and product development. Both also set up a separate customer development team, responsible for relations with retailers across all the companies' brands. ...

Ever since the 1950s, when they were developed by American manufacturers of fast-moving consumer goods, marketing departments have revolved around brand managers. Companies such as Procter & Gamble developed brands that divided markets into ever-narrower segments (not just shampoo, but anti-dandruff shampoo). Each brand manager was responsible for a single brand in a single country, handling matters such as advertising and packaging. A separate sales department was responsible for getting products onto retailers' shelves.

1 Which two expressions are used in the second headline and the first paragraph to talk about the closure of marketing departments?

conglomerate 11 ⇑

2 If you focus on something, you c o n _ _ _ _ _ _ _ a t e on it.

3 If you divide a market into ever-narrower segments, do the segments get more and more specialized?

This time-tested structure is now facing unprecedented questioning in its FMCG heartland. A recent study of American consumer-goods firms by the Boston Consulting Group found that 90% of those surveyed claimed to have restructured their marketing departments. ...

People buy goods increasingly on price, not because they carry a famous name. This was driven home to advertising men on April 2nd 1993, when Philip Morris announced that it would slash the price of Marlboro cigarettes to defend the much advertised brand from cheap, generic rivals whose share of America's cigarette market had jumped to 36% from 28% in nine months. 'Marlboro Friday' prompted analysts to proclaim the death of brands, though it may be that Philip Morris had pushed up Marlboro's price too far. ...

Another trend is the shift of power from manufacturers to retailers. Investment in new shops and information technology, and the weakening in the power of brands, have helped retailers to exploit their proximity to the consumer and dictate terms to their suppliers. Sales of own-label goods continue to rise, pushing branded goods from the shelves, especially if they are not leaders in their category.

Has all this made marketing too important to be left to the marketing department? A recent study by the London branch of Coopers & Lybrand, an accountancy firm, concluded that 'marketing as a discipline is more vital than ever' but that the marketing department itself is 'critically ill'.

And in an essay last year, consultants at McKinsey argued that large marketing departments are often 'a millstone around an organisation's neck'. Many companies that have 're-engineered' their production departments are now applying the same process-driven logic to their marketing department. ...

4 If something is unprecedented, has it happened before?

restructuring *22* ⇑

5 If the price of something is slashed, is it reduced
a) a lot, or
b) a little?

6 If a retailer dictates terms to its suppliers, are the suppliers in a position to negotiate with the retailer?

supplier *71* ⇑

7 If someone or something is critically ill, are they seriously ill?

8 'A millstone round your neck' is a way of talking about a h a n d i _ _ _ _ .

re-engineering *48, 75* ⇑

Crossword

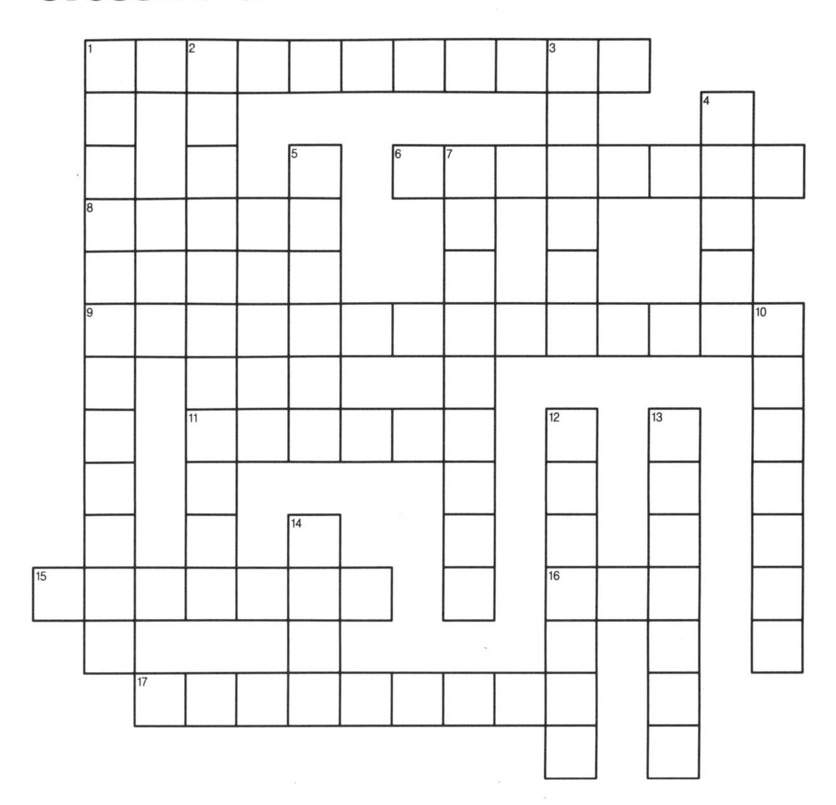

Across

1 and 7 down. What you have if you're ahead of your competitors (11,9)
6 and 14 down. The direct marketeer's ______ is the recipient's ______ mail. (8, 4)
8 'Nice' to have if, as a marketeer, you can find one: add an 'h'. (5)
9 Marketeers like to get this recognition. (5, 9)
11 and 17. This approach cuts out the retailer (6, 9)
15 Sales turnover: here it's singular, but it can be plural (7)
16 and 13 down. Main competitors, not only in the sports goods market (3, 7)

Down

1 When a company's products take sales from one another, they get ______ (12)
2 Goods as a noun, and presenting them as a verb (11)
3 The quantity sold is the sales ______ (6)
4 Products unusual in the singular (5)
5 One with the biggest market share (6)
7 See 1 across
10 A slice of the market (7)
12 If you bundle goods together and sell them as one unit, you get a ______ (7)
13 See 16 across
14 See 6 across

Sales

sales
- sales figures
- sales revenue
- sales revenues
- sales target
- sales turnover
- sales volume
- unit sales

revenue stream

Businesses live or die, of course, by their **sales**.

A salesperson's or organization's **sales target** is the number or value of goods that they hope to sell in a given period.

Sales figures show **unit sales**, the number of goods sold, and **sales revenue**, **sales revenues**, or **sales turnover**, the money resulting from these sales.

Sales volume, confusingly, can mean either unit sales: the number of goods sold, or sales revenues.

When considering revenues over time, commentators talk about the **revenue stream** that a business or product generates.

◆ **LANGUAGE NOTE**

Do not confuse the noun **sale** with the verb **sell, sold, sold**: if you make a sale, you sell something.
Do not confuse **sales** in this context with **sale** used to talk about a period when prices are reduced temporarily.
Turnover referring to sales is used mainly in British English.

Safeway's sales figures are a closely guarded commercial secret.

Although passenger cars produced half the company's sales revenue, in relation to the other world-wide manufacturers of cars, Volvo was quite small.

Despite higher unit sales, revenues from IBM's PC business fell too, thanks to a fierce price war.

After only a month, the company reached its annual sales target of Pert-Plus shampoo in Poland.

Zantac is the world's best-selling drug and the source of 44 per cent of Glaxo's £4 billion annual turnover.

Mapco estimated sales volume for the two firms at about 17 million tons of coal.

...Random House, the largest trade publishing house in the US. The company said the publisher's annual sales volume increased to $800 million from $40 million during Mr Bernstein's tenure.

Allowing cable television companies to also offer cable telephony services provides them with an important early second revenue stream which many analysts now believe will eventually overtake cable television revenues themselves.

1 **Sales logic.** Which word is missing from all these extracts? In which extracts is it singular, and in which plural?

world markets for at least five years. The minimum sales .... of 200 coaches per year would net up to £75 million
market is also seen as important. The Amstrad sales .... is the 80 per cent of the possible user population that it
after only a month, the company reached its annual sales .... for Pert shampoo in Poland. When large multinationals
None will be of any use unless meet-or-beat sales .... can be established. He admits this is difficult for newly
with a view to developing exports and reviving sales .... nearer to the 300 vehicles a week achieved last year.
touted anti-anemia compound. Analysts' first year sales .... of the drug are in the $100 million, but some think they
groups of employees set their own productivity and sales .... There are no controls over travel or business expenses.

Costs and cost-cutting

cost structure

costs
- fixed costs
- variable costs
- direct costs
- indirect costs
- overhead costs

overheads

The money that a business spends in order to produce goods or services is its **costs**. Businesses of different kinds have different **cost structures** and define, calculate, and refer to their costs in different ways.

Fixed costs do not vary in relation to the output level of goods or services; **variable costs** do, as the example illustrates.

output 68 ⇑

Direct costs are directly related to the things produced. In manufacturing, for example, direct costs include raw materials and wages and **indirect costs** may include things like social security charges on top of the wages.

raw materials 71 ⇑
labour 43 ⇑

Overhead costs or **overheads** are used to mean different things, but usually cover all the regular non-production costs of running a business, such as salaries and telephone bills, and can be extended, for example, to include the cost of marketing and R&D activities.

Lufthansa's cost problem is illustrated in a comparison with British Airways, where personnel costs amount to about 24 per cent of revenues against Lufthansa's 33 per cent. Lufthansa insists that the agreement contributes considerably to making the cost structure of Lufthansa internationally more competitive.

Mr Shilling contends that in its quest to get 'lean and mean', US industry has exchanged variable costs for fixed costs. Many of the blue-collar workers who used to make things have been replaced by more productive machines, usually financed by debt. But while blue-collar workers could be laid off when recession occurred, machines can't be fired, and interest payments don't go away.

blue-collar workers 43 ⇑
fire 46 ⇑
lay off 52 ⇑
recession 178 ⇓

Firms locate their production and other operations internationally for reasons that are more complex than the simple minimisation of direct costs.

Mainly because of higher indirect costs, a German manufacturing worker costs almost twice as much per hour as a British one.

manufacturing *67* ⇑

...marketing, research and all the other things that distinguish a firm from a factory. Apple had come to spend a lot on such things. Its selling, general and administrative expenses (i.e. non-manufacturing overheads) made up 32% of sales.

firm *1* ⇑
factory *67* ⇑

2 **Cost-cutting exercise.** Managers describe plans to cut costs in predictable ways. Complete the words on the right meaning 'plan' and those on the left describing the severity of the plans.

s _ v _ r _		m _ _ s u r _
d r _ s t _ c		p r _ g r _ m m _
s t r _ n g _ n t	**cost-cutting**	_ x _ r c _ s _
h _ g _		c _ m p _ _ g n
_ g g r _ s s _ v _		s c h _ m _

Expenses and expenditure

expenses
expenditure
spend
 marketing spend
 overspend
budget

Costs are also referred to as **expenses** or **expenditure**.

Spend, until recently only used as a verb, is now also used as a noun in expressions like **marketing spend** and in noun compounds like **overspend**.

Planned expenditure is shown, **budgeted**, or **budgeted for** in a **budget**.

Rising operating expenses are another problem. Fuel costs were up 10% in the third quarter and labor costs are on the upswing again at many carriers.

Japanese and American retail demand for diamonds is soft, despite an intensified advertising and marketing campaign launched by De Beers earlier this year. The group's marketing spend in 1992 is budgeted at $164 million.

marketing *110* ⇑

Jaguar's R&D expenditure and advertising expenditure are still at very low levels compared to those of Mercedes Benz and BMW.

R&D *59* ⇑
advertising *104* ⇑

Yesterday it was revealed that the BBC budgeted for cuts in costs of resources, such as studios, yet to be made. Computer error has also contributed to the overspend.

Derek Lewis, who is heading the launch of UK Gold said the channel would be launched with a £3 million promotional budget.

launch 86 ⇑
promotion 106 ⇑

3 Spend function. The word 'spend' has been omitted from these extracts. Where does it go in each extract? In which of the extracts is 'spend' used as a verb, and in which as a noun?

1. 15,000 to 20,000 companies have five or more locations. Together, these companies an estimated $12 billion annually on telecommunications services.
2. Advertisers $2 billion a year in the production of commercials.
3. It takes great courage to maintain a high marketing in a downturn.
4. Not for nothing do drug companies more than £1 million on medical journal advertising.
5. Radio takes only 2% of Britain's total advertising.
6. Some companies months carrying out market research before launching a magazine.
7. The necessary increase in marketing may mean profits slip a little in the second half.

advertising 104 ⇑

Economies of scale and the learning curve

economies of scale

unit cost

experience curve
learning curve

Economies of scale is the theory that the larger the size of a production unit, the lower the **unit cost**: the cost of producing one ton of coal, one car, or one package holiday for example.

The notion of the **learning curve** or **experience curve** is that the more an individual or organization does something, the more quickly and efficiently they do it, and its cost declines correspondingly.

The arrival of the package holiday coincided with the onset of mass air travel, and the economies of scale of huge hotel complexes on the coasts of southern Europe.

British Coal has already shut the most unprofitable mines; and most of those that remain have costs similar to each others'. So further contraction could actually increase unit costs, as the overheads would be spread over fewer mines.

The Boston Consulting Group calls this the experience curve. Some of the reasons suggested for this by the BCG are: a) the learning function. Anyone doing a job learns to do it better over time and, given increased experience, labour costs should in fact decline by about 10 to 15 per cent each time cumulative production doubles. …

Newspapers and magazines are still feeling their way in the electronic world. 'We're going to be shaping the service as we go along,' says Victor Perry, vice president of new business development of the 'Los Angeles Times'. 'This is new to us. We don't pretend to have all the answers, but it's important to get on the learning curve now. Newspapers without on-line services will be left behind.'

4 Diseconomies of scale. Read this extract from *The Economist* and answer the questions.

THE FALL OF BIG BUSINESS

... 'Big' no longer means, as it once did, 'successful'; before long it is likely to mean 'failing'. If this prediction seems too bleak, recall how rosy the outlook seemed for big firms ten years ago. When globalisation became a cliché, businessmen assumed that big firms would gain the most from lower trade barriers and converging tastes. Global markets, it seemed, would call for global brands from global companies managed globally. Firms big enough to spend lavishly on automated factories and computerised offices would be able to exploit glittering new technologies faster than smaller, and poorer rivals. ... Many pundits confidently forecast that a handful of giant firms would dominate car making, electronics, banking, entertainment, advertising and publishing, to name only a few.

At the time, such predictions seemed plausible. For decades firms in almost every business had sought 'economies of scale', the idea that manufacturing or distributing goods in ever larger volumes lowers cost per unit, so that a firm becomes more efficient as it grows. Most managers also recognised that expanding a business also involves new costs. As they grow, firms may become more bureaucratic, inflexible and wasteful.

1 Which two adjectives with opposite meanings are used here to talk about the future?

2 If consumer tastes converge, do they become more similar or less similar?

brand *91* ⇑

3 A pundit is an e x _ _ _ _ who is asked to give their opinion in the media.

advertising *104* ⇑

4 If a prediction is plausible, is it credible?

Employees, believing themselves to be mere cogs, are less accountable and harder to motivate. But such diseconomies were usually a footnote. They seemed more than outweighed by the benefits of bigness. The triumphs of mass production early in the century had given birth to most of the giant firms which came to tower over their industries. That bigger was better was rarely disputed. Until recently it was even true. The great surprise of the last decade has been that the changes which were supposed to make bigger even better have had the opposite effect. ...

A blow to big firms is that the use of computers, confounding most forecasts, is narrowing economies of scale in manufacturing and distribution, not expanding them. Factory automation is making it possible to produce goods cheaply in smaller volumes. The plummeting price of computers is enabling smaller firms to employ the same logistical techniques, sophisticated financial models, and automated payrolls and other administrative tasks that were available only to big firms in the past. ...

5 Powerless people in an organization complain about being cogs in a m a c _ _ _ _ _.

mass production 67 ⇑

6 If someone or something towers over something, they d o m _ _ _ _ _ _ it.

7 If a forecast is confounded, is it proved right?

automation 69 ⇑

8 If a price plummets, does it fall by a small amount?

plummet 167 ⇓

payroll 43 ⇑

Into profit

margin
- gross margin
- profit margin
- net margin

mark-up

profitability

Companies in different businesses define **gross margin** in various ways, but it is often the difference between the selling price of goods and their production cost, without taking into account other costs such as marketing and general overheads.

A company's or product's **profit margin** is the difference between its total costs and its sales revenues. This profit margin may be referred to as **net margin** to distinguish it from gross margin.

Margin is expressed as a percentage of the selling price. It can also be expressed as a percentage of the total cost of goods: in this case it is referred to as the **mark-up**.

These are measures of a product's or a business's **profitability**.

Because fixed costs are high and variable costs low, any gain in market share fattens profits.

market share 83 ⇑

Gross margin is the money that Apple has left after paying the costs of making its product.

Frank Farrant, Pentland's finance director, said the first task would be to increase Adidas's dismal profitability, from a present net margin of about 1 per cent to about 10 per cent in two or three years' time.

If they can sell the potatoes, they get 3p a pound, while they retail at 15p a pound. 'Supermarkets are getting a huge mark-up, while we have to sell at a price that doesn't even cover costs,' said one Essex farmer.

break even
break even point

return on investment
ROI

contribution

When sales reach a level where revenues match costs, a company or product **breaks even**. This is **break even** or the **break even point**, a crucial figure when calculating the **return on investment** or **ROI** for a given business or product.

The **contribution** generated by each product in a product line or by each business in a group is the amount it represents in terms of overall profit.

◆ **LANGUAGE NOTE**

The noun **break even** is also spelled with a hyphen and as one word.

BSkyB broke even a year ago and is now making an operating profit of £1.7 million a week on weekly revenues of £7 million.

With the British, Italian and Spanish aerospace companies keeping the costs down, and with 450 aircraft shared between the three partner air forces, the cost per aircraft could still come out at £21 million. Financial break-even point for the project is 400 aircraft.

The project entailed setting up a software development division – a cost that could not be justified unless Servasure could license the system to others when it was completed. Harper predicted a seven-year haul before there was a chance of a return on investment.

All three divisions within the group increased their contribution to profits, including the main packaging business, still responsible for about 70 per cent of the whole.

5 Cost, sales, and profit logic. Complete this article from the *Guardian* with the listed expressions. (a occurs twice and the others once each.)

a costs
b gross margin
c overheads
d expenses
e sales
f profit margin

WHY CDs ARE MUSIC TO THE EARS AT POLYGRAM

...Polygram's labels, which include Decca, Deutsche Grammophon, A&M, Polydor, Island, Mercury and London, clocked up no fewer than 24 albums which sold 1 million copies or more: its biggest selling release was Billy Ray Cyrus's album, *Some Gave All*, which sold more than 7 million copies. ...

With effect from the beginning of last year, the company acquired a CD factory from Philips (its 80 per cent parent). With Polygram's existing CD plants in France and Germany, the group manufactured about 70 per cent of its output in-house. This helped improve the group's gross margin to just over 47 per cent. (At this point, those with a CD player who feel they are being ripped off when they are forced to spend £12.99 for a disc, prick up your ears.) Polygram does not break down the margin it makes on each of its businesses. But the overall picture is intriguing.

parent company 11 ⇑
output 68 ⇑
in-house 71 ⇑

Expressed in Dutch currency, Polygram's sales last year were 6.6 billion guilders. What Polygram calls 'direct __________ (1) of sales' amounted to 3.5 billion guilders: these direct costs included manufacturing __________ (2), royalties to artists, copyright fees, things like that. Take costs from __________ (3) revenues and you have 3.1 billion guilders, which gives the __________ __________ (4) figure of 47 per cent. (Buyers of CDs start reddening in the face. A profit margin of 47 per cent? Much muttering of 'extortion' and 'daylight robbery'.) But of that 3.1 billion guilders of gross income, all but 790 million is gobbled up by 'selling __________ (5)', for which read marketing and distribution, and general administration expenses.

So the net __________ __________ (6) appears to be a rather more reasonable 11.9 per cent, if one accepts that it is right that 28 per cent of sales should be taken up in marketing and distribution and a further 8 per cent in general __________ (7). And as Polygram's president Alain Levy pointed out yesterday, at the moment less than 0.2 per cent of consumer spending goes on music. There is plenty of scope for growth, even if we moan about having to spend £12.99 on a CD.

Shipping the goods

order place an order trade dispatch ship invoice bill invoicing billing pay up front

When a customer **orders** or **places an order** for goods from a supplier, the supplier **invoices** or **bills** the customer for these goods. Producing and sending invoices is known as **invoicing** or **billing**.

customer 79 ⇑
supplier 71 ⇑

If a customer pays for goods before they are **shipped** or **dispatched**, they **pay up front.**

Ship has an additional meaning in American English. If a product will ship at a specified time, it will become available for customers at that time.

◆ **LANGUAGE NOTE**

Dispatch is also spelled **despatch** in British English.
The verb **ship** does not necessarily indicate the use of a ship to transport goods.
Invoice and **bill** are also nouns: see the exercise below.

The future of the former Leyland DAF truck plant in Lancashire looked more secure last night after British Telecom announced that it had placed an order worth £8.2 million for 206 trucks.

You consult the electronic brochure, place your order and it is billed to your credit card. The goods are automatically dispatched from the US, which at current exchange rates can be extremely cost-effective.

'Harvey started billing me four times more than he should have,' Mr Trump says. 'The bills were too high and I wasn't satisfied.'

In one of a series of expensive errors a government department received a bill for £6,100 instead of £61 for the toilet repair. The errors in invoicing for work at public offices have cost millions of pounds.

When he was contacted by a Taiwanese firm interested in his products, he thought it was a joke. 'I invoiced them expecting to hear nothing more,' he said. 'But they wrote back and paid £30,000 for part of the deal up front.

... continental brick producers, who shipped bricks to Britain during the boom of the late 1980s.

IBM announced version 2.2 of OS/2 this week. It will ship late next month.

6 Margin for error? Read this article from *The Times* and match the listed trading documents to their descriptions.

1	purchase order	a	payment document issued by customer's bank
2	invoice	b	confirmation from supplier to customer that goods have been sent
3	banker's order	c	confirmation that payment has been made, giving form of payment
4	shipping advice or dispatch note	d	details from customer of goods sent, the sum owed by the supplier, and conditions of payment
5	remittance advice	e	request for goods from a customer to a supplier

HEY PRESTO FOR BUSINESS

Electronic data interchange could change the face of trading in Britain.

Anyone who has been promised that 'the cheque is in the post' knows the problems of paper-based trading. Even when the cheque finally arrives it may be payable to the wrong person or filled in for an incorrect amount. From invoices and shipping advices to remittances and banker's orders, the problems are the same: paper can be slow, unwieldy and prone to error.

Now technology is coming to the rescue, with a computerised trading technique known as Electronic Data Interchange (EDI), which is faster, cheaper and more accurate. The idea emerged in the mid 1980s, when computers and telecommunications equipment had been installed in companies for a wide range of activities, from production and distribution to accounts and marketing.

Extending computer links beyond the company was the next logical step. This enables a retailer to place electronic orders with a supplier, who can then transmit a shipping advice note when the goods are dispatched. Invoices can also be generated automatically. ...

Speed is a big bonus. Data sent by post and processed manually can take days or even weeks. EDI takes less time than sealing an envelope, so orders can be placed and confirmed in seconds. By eliminating manual processes, EDI reduces the possibility for mistakes. Research shows that around 70 per cent of information being entered into computers has previously been printed out by other computers. At each stage, inaccuracies may creep in. Some 40 per cent of the invoices sent or received by European companies contain errors, and the statistics for inaccurate purchase orders and dispatch notes are just as bad. ...

Getting paid

trade credit

accounts payable
accounts receivable
payables
receivables

creditors
debtors

cash flow

A company supplying goods or services to another company does not, of course, usually expect to be paid immediately, but after an agreed period. This is **trade credit**.

customer 79 ⇑
supplier 71 ⇑

Amounts that a business is waiting to be paid by its customers are **accounts receivable** or **receivables**. Customers owing money in this way are **debtors**.

Money that a business owes to its suppliers are **accounts payable** or **payables**. Suppliers waiting to be paid are **creditors**.

The **cash flow** of a business is the actual movement of money into and out of it, independently of how much it owes and is owed.

Cash flow is also used to refer exclusively to cash flowing into a company from sales, as in the last example.

◆ **LANGUAGE NOTE**

Cash flow is also spelled with a hyphen or as one word.

'There's nothing strange about the reaction of suppliers, because this company hasn't been the best corporate citizen in terms of payment,' said Sanford Sigoloff, the new chief executive of LJ Hooker. 'Our job is essentially to work with the trade, give them cash before delivery, and then develop a relationship that allows them to give us trade credit.'

Intent on controlling costs, Friedsam instituted a strict accounts-receivable system, cutting average collection time by more than half, to 40 days.

Mr Derita said his company is waiting to receive payment on September payables before it allows any of its manufacturers to ship new merchandise to Federated and Allied.

merchandise 85 ⇑

Small businesses would routinely tell her they had receivables of thousands of dollars but no accounts payable.

The latest of the Small Business Research Trust's authoritative reports shows that the problem of cashflow, payments and debtors remains the most serious one for small firms, after low turnover and lack of business.

Wall Street analysts generally estimate that Time Warner can generate cash flow of $2 million a year.

7 **Cash flow logic.** Complete this extract from the *Financial Times* with the items listed. (One of the expressions is used twice, five are used once each and two are not used.)

a	cash flow	c	profitability	e	bill	g	sales
b	cash up front	d	trade credit	f	receivables	h	turnover

CONTROLLING THE CASH FLOW

...About half Exitech's __________ (1) comes from __________ (2) of the 7000 series machine. Gower and Rumsby are grateful that the percentage is no higher. Manufacturing such expensive machines creates problems of __________ (3).

'__________ (4), even for a machine that might cost £500,000, is something that large multinationals are reluctant to supply to a small company on the other side of the world,' he said.

'We have to live with this. We have had sticky moments when building a machine that costs £400,000 and face an immediate __________ (5) of half that amount for buying in components. However, the bank is usually sympathetic when we are in a difficult __________ (6) situation.

'They have no doubts over our __________ (7), and have the comfort of knowing that we own our three buildings outright.

'There are many laser producers who would like to work closely with us, and we have good relationships with biomedical and electronic end users. It's nice to be liked.'

end-user
101 ⇑

In the red

'Yes. But not as far in debt as a young company like yours should be!'

overdraft
in the red

financing

security

debtor

working capital
tie up working capital

liquidity

cash injection
cash infusion

A business with cash flow difficulties may ask its bank for an **overdraft**: their account at the bank is then **in the red**. This is a form of **financing** from the bank (and an expensive one), and the business's receivables are **security** for this financing.

Working capital is money used to bridge the gap between the time products are planned, materials are paid for and the goods produced, and the time payment is received for them from customers when they are sold. By getting hold of money that it is owed sooner, a company reduces the working capital it has **tied up** in debtors.

A firm without sufficient working capital has **liquidity** problems and may look for a **cash injection** or a **cash infusion**.

Alastair West's independent company was faced two years ago with a demand from its bankers to cut its overdraft by a third within 48 hours, in spite of the fact that after 20 years in business it was still trading profitably. Not only that, the security backing the overdraft was still worth more than double the funds it was covering. It all occurred at the time when, as Mr West grimly observes, banks were running round 'like headless chickens'.

While British bankers talk of being in the red because of the old practice of showing overdrawn accounts in red ink, Italians talk about being in the green.

The survey highlighted the problem of late payment across Europe, not only in Britain, but the factoring association reports an improvement, with the average time to collect debts falling to 57 days from 62 days at the beginning of the year, the first time it has fallen below 60 days for five years.

Research showed that 54 percent of firms had no form of financial plan which included budgets and cash-flow analysis. Mr Lavarack says that because most small firms are sales-driven, they do not take into account either the profitability of their product or service, or the working capital required to finance increased sales. As a result, businesses may find that as trading increases, they are selling their goods at lower prices than necessary, and experiencing difficulties as their cash is tied up in increased stocks and debtors.

Campeau said Federated and Allied need cash infusions to meet 'liquidity needs'. They include working capital to buy inventory and funds to pay bond interest due tomorrow.

bonds *148* ⇓

There are lots of ways liquidity could be injected into small companies if the will was there. It could take the form of low (or delayed) interest loans from the government.

8 **Overdraft alternatives.** A number of words are missing from this article from the *Financial Times*. Where does each of the listed expressions occur? (They occur once each in the order listed: a, b, c, d, e and f in the second paragraph, and g and h in the third.)

a financed	c factoring	e debtor	g security
b bank overdraft	d debts	f collection	h receivable

FACTORING'S UNSUNG ROLE FOR EXPORTERS

An overdraft is not the only option for companies trading overseas.

Eddie George, governor of the Bank of England, gave factoring a generous 'plug' at a dinner in London last week. Yet for all the publicity which this form of finance now receives, a surprising number of businesses, notably exporters, remain ignorant of its charms.

Around 85 per cent of UK exports are still by the traditional, despite the advantages of using companies – which buy in return for an immediate cash payment, take over records and provide a service for clients.

Overdrafts, indeed, are seldom used effectively to finance overseas trade. Most banks seek for loans, often using a company's assets including its trade debts to support any overdraft. They will usually lend up to 60 per cent of the value of a current UK, but they still will not lend anything against the value of foreign trade debts.

This leads to the absurd situation where a company might be given no credit on the back of an export sale to, say, a leading multinational conglomerate – but would be advanced up to 60 per cent of the value of a sale to a small corner shop. ...

multinational *2* ⇑

conglomerate *11* ⇑

Servicing debt

borrower
lender

loan
borrowing
lending
indebtedness

debt
short-term
medium-term
long-term

default on a debt

interest
interest rate

principal

Depending on whether you are a **borrower**, such as a business in need of finance, or a **lender**, such as a bank, you may describe a **loan** as **borrowing**, **lending**, or **debt**.

The state of being in debt is **indebtedness**.

Interest for a loan is charged at a percentage **rate**. The **principal** is the amount originally lent.

Debt is **short-term** if it is to be repaid over a few months or years or **medium-** or **long-term** if over a longer period.

If a company fails to make debt repayments on time, or at all, it **defaults** on the debt.

◆ **LANGUAGE NOTE**

The forms **borrowings** and **lendings** exist, but **lendings** is quite rare.

In Japan, the lending bank and the borrower are often part of the same associated group of companies. This close connection between lender and borrower makes it easier for the firm to convince the borrower to contribute additional capital and help the firm sort out its problems if things go wrong.

Corporate indebtedness rose sharply in the boom years of the late 1980s.

In short-term planning, the planning horizon is rarely longer than the next 12 months. The firm wants to make sure it has enough cash to pay its bills, and that short-term borrowing and lending are arranged to the best advantage.

The growth in earnings had let the company get ahead of schedule in repaying long-term debt, which had been raised from $19 million to $302 million. It is now 18 months early in repaying the principal on its seven-year bank loan.

earnings *162* ⇓

Mr Dunlop, the chairman, said, 'The interest bill for a company of this size is far too high. Short term borrowings are £37 million.' He said the 1 per cent interest rate cut was worth £500,000 a year to profitability.

Washington Public Power Supply System (WPPSS) which owns the dubious honor of the biggest municipal bond default in history said its proposed refunding has been rescheduled for after Labor Day. WPPSS earned its Wall Street nickname Whoops when it defaulted on roughly one-fourth of the more than $8 billion of bonds it sold in the 1970s and early 1980s to build five nuclear power plants.

bonds *148* ⇓

9 **Partners in debt.** Find combinations in the box used to talk about:

1 paying loans back to the lender. (two expressions)
2 re-negotiating the form of debts.
3 re-negotiating the dates that debts are to be re-paid.
4 the overall amount of an organization's debt.
5 a period when a debtor is having trouble repaying their debts.

	a) repayment	
f) servicing		b) burden
	debt	
e) restructuring		c) rescheduling
	d) crisis	

Now choose correct forms of these words to complete the extracts, choosing between the alternatives suggested in each case. (For example, the word missing in i is either b or e.)

i The aircraft leasing company owes $5.5 billion, and is deeply embroiled in debt-__________ (b, e) talks with shareholders, bankers and aircraft manufacturers.

shareholders 9 ⇑
manufacturers 67 ⇑

ii But the biggest danger of all lies in the huge corporate debt __________ (b, c). A prolonged period of falling prices raises the real level of that debt, and makes it harder for companies to __________ (d, f) it. It is a sobering thought on the golf courses around Tokyo. Many of the courses were built in the boom years of the late 1980s, on the back of huge borrowings. Falling green fees may be good news for golfers, but the courses need more revenue, not less, to meet their debt-__________ (b, f) costs.

boom 176 ⇓
demand 178 ⇓

iii Stronger demand will lift Forte's profits, while lower interest rates will cut the cost of its debt __________ . (a, d)

iv Though there is pressure across the British banking industry to take a tough line on loans, bankers will __________ debts if they can see some hope. (c, f)

v Ten years ago, Mexico's announcement that it could not __________ (a, f) its debt launched the 1980s debt __________ (c, d). Today, Mexico's public debt __________ (b, d), successfully renegotiated, is a smaller proportion of the country's wealth than that of most industrialized countries.

Assets

assets
current assets
fixed assets
intangible assets

depreciate
amortize
depreciation
amortization
book value

charge

goodwill

going concern

Things of value or earning power to a firm are its **assets.**

Current assets include cash, receivables, bank deposits, and trade investments: investments in other companies.

Fixed assets include land, plant, buildings, and furniture. Assets such as plant and equipment that over time wear out or become outdated are said to **depreciate.** A **charge** must be made for this **depreciation** or **amortization** in calculating a business's profitability: the assets are **depreciated** or **amortized** by an amount each year.

The **book value** of an item of equipment is the amount it is theoretically worth after depreciation, but this may not reflect what someone would pay for it if it was sold.

Intangible assets may include such things as patents owned by the company, and **goodwill**, the value of the company as a functioning business or **going concern** with a client base, experienced management, and other benefits that a start-up may not have.

start-up *28* ⇑

◆ **LANGUAGE NOTE**

Amortize and **amortization** are also spelled **amortise** and **amortisation** in British English, where, in any case, the terms **depreciate** and **depreciation** are usually preferred.

The figures revealed that News Corp's debt had blown out to A$10.5 billion and that current assets of A$3.4 billion were little more than half current liabilities of $6 billion.

Goodwill is an asset: the value of a firm as going concern in excess of the sum of its parts.

The need for an asset to be 'measured at a monetary amount with sufficient reliability' would also affect accounting for intangible assets such as brand names.

brand *91* ⇑

Mr Agnelli said the group remains fully committed to its heavy investment programme. This saw combined spending on fixed assets and research and development rise to 8.2 trillion lire from 6.7 trillion a year earlier.

British Airports Authority has expanded the 'economic life' of its terminals and runways from 16 years and 23.5 years respectively to 50 years for terminals and 100 years for runways. This means these assets can be depreciated over a longer period, reducing the annual charge, and thereby increasing reported profits.

The technology is developing so fast that Rebo's High Definition Television, which it had initially planned on amortizing over five years, grew obsolete in less than two years. Now Rebo must lay out money for a newer, even costlier generation of equipment.

The book value of a catalytic cracker may be a poor guide to its true value, but at least you know what cash in the bank is worth.

10 **Can brands be valued as intangible assets?** Arrange these sections from a *Financial Times* article into a logical order. (a is the first paragraph and g is the last.)

IBM PLUNGES TO BOTTOM OF BRAND NAME VALUE LEAGUE

a IBM has plunged in one year from the third most valuable brand name in the world to the bottom of a league table of 290 brands, according to an annual survey that attempts the controversial task of evaluating 'what's in a name'.

b To that figure it applies a 'brand strength' multiple based on factors such as market position, degree of internationalisation and trends in the sector. Using the formula – which was originally developed by Interbrand, the UK-based brand consultancy – the value of the Compaq name climbed 149 per cent in 1993 to a value of $4 billion and a league table position of 21, compared with a position of 65 in 1992.

c The survey, to be published by the US magazine *Financial World*, uses a complex formula to arrive at its rankings. After breaking down company earnings by brand, it then subtracts what it calculates would be earned on a basic, unbranded version of the product.

earnings 162 ⇓

d Meanwhile, IBM's name now has a negative value, says *Financial World*. That means that plant and equipment expenses and taxes wiped out any brand earnings. Other brands falling into this 'negative worth' category include: Del Monte, Siemens, Corning, Krups, Moulinex, Michelin and Pirelli. The magazine says: 'A competing generic product could have generated higher profits on the same level of sales.'

generic product 91 ⇑

e Evaluating brands, and attempting to capitalise them as intangible assets on balance sheets, is a controversial area. Last week Sir Michael Perry, chairman of Unilever, the Anglo-Dutch consumer products group, criticised 'fancy brand accounting' in a speech in London to the Advertising Association.

f Coca-Cola is ranked number one in the league table, with a brand name worth nearly $36 billion (£23.6 billion) followed by Marlboro at $33 billion, Nescafe $12 billion, Kodak $10 billion and Microsoft $10 billion.

g 'The seemingly miraculous conjuring up of intangible asset values, as if from nowhere, only serves to reinforce the view of the consumer sceptics, that brands are just about high prices and consumer exploitation. At Unilever we have consistently rejected this approach,' he said. ...

Liabilities

liabilities
long-term liabilities
current liabilities

gearing
leverage
highly geared
highly leveraged

Debts to lenders form part of a company's **liabilities**.

Liabilities is also used to refer exclusively to debt. Long-term debts are **long-term liabilities**.

The ratio of a firm's debt to its equity is its **gearing** or **leverage**; a firm with a high proportion of debt in relation to equity is **highly geared** or **highly leveraged**.

equity *163* ⇓

Short-term debts and debts to suppliers are among its **current liabilities**.

◆ **LANGUAGE NOTE**

The term **gearing** is used mainly in British English and **leverage** in American English.

Any buyer of USX would have to assume $5.8 billion in debt, plus billions more in other liabilities.

Current liabilities are bills that the company expects to pay in the near future. They include debts that are due to be repaid within the next year and payables: amounts owed by the company to its suppliers. In addition to these short-term obligations, International Paper has issued bonds that will not be repaid for many years. These are shown as long-term liabilities.

bonds *148* ⇓

Joe Dwyer, Wimpey's chief executive, said: 'We are in a good debt position and although gearing will rise, it is controllable.'

When a firm borrows money, it promises to make a series of fixed payments. Because the shareholders get only what is left over after the debtholders have been paid, debt is said to create financial leverage.

A company may be too highly geared for the realities of the markets in which it is operating.

Investors worry that an economic downturn would make it difficult for highly leveraged companies to meet their debt obligations.

downturn *176* ⇓

11 **Leverage logic.** Complete this extract about leverage with the words listed. (a occurs four times, b three times, c and d twice each, and the others once each.)

a debt
b assets
c leverage
d market
e debtholders
f accounting

LEVERAGING THE ASSETS

Financial __________ (1) is usually measured by the ratio of long-term debt to total long-term capital. Another way to express leverage is in terms of the company's debt-equity ratio. Notice that both these measures make use of book, i.e. __________ (2), values rather than market values.

The market value of a company finally determines whether __________ (3) get their money back, so you would expect analysts to look at the face amount of the __________ (4) as a proportion of the total market value of the __________ (5) and equity. The main reason they don't do this is that __________ (6) values are not readily available. Does it matter much? Perhaps not; after all, the __________ (7) value includes the value of intangible assets generated by research and development, advertising, staff training and so on. These __________ (8) are not readily saleable and, if the company falls on hard times, the value of these __________ (9) may fall to zero. For some purposes, it may be just as well to follow the accountant and to ignore these intangible __________ (10) entirely.

Notice also that this measure of __________ (11) takes account only of long-term __________ (12) obligations. Managers sometimes also define __________ (13) to include all liabilities other than equity. …

capital *163* ⇓
equity *163* ⇓

Reporting results

'Good grief! This balance sheet won't do – why damn it, a child could understand it.'

balance sheet
off-balance sheet
strong balance sheet
weak balance sheet

provision
bad debts

write off

Assets and liabilities are normally shown on a firm's **balance sheet**: a 'photograph' taken, normally once a year, of its financial situation at that time.

Firms in a good situation are said to have a **strong balance sheet** and those that are not, a **weak** one.

Things that are not shown in the balance sheet but in a footnote, for example, are **off-balance sheet**.

A company's balance sheet may include **provisions** for potential losses, such as **bad debts**, debts that may never be paid. If it looks almost certain that a debt will not be paid, it is considered a **write-off** and **written off**.

◆ **LANGUAGE NOTE**

Off-balance sheet is also spelled **off-balance-sheet**.
Provisions are **reserves** in American English. Do not confuse this with the British English meaning of **reserves**.

reserves *163* ⇓

Total has a strong balance sheet: debt has fallen from 37% of equity to 25% since 1989.

Unlike Toyota, which is known as the 'Toyota Bank' because of the huge pile of cash on which it sits, Nissan still has a weak balance sheet.

Another frequently quoted term in modern accounting is 'off-balance sheet'. Assets as well as liabilities are removed from the balance sheet of the company concerned, and there may also be some impact on the profit-and-loss account. But the usual aim is to reduce a company's apparent gearing.

At Lloyd's Bank, bad debt provisions fell by almost £100 million to £329 million, helped by an improvement in Third World country debts.

Bankers Trust New York Corp reported a third-quarter loss of $1.72 billion following its $1.6 billion boost in reserves for losses on loans to less-developed countries.

The collapse of Citygrove, the property developer, was partly responsible for a £3.15 million bad debts write-off at Henry Barrett, the steel and industrial products company.

The ministry is allowing banks to pretend that bad debts remain good, in order to keep their profits up. In time though, many bad loans will have to be written off, further depleting capital.

results
report results

profit
loss
pre-tax profit
pre-tax loss

profit and loss account
income statement

accounts
accountants
auditors

creative accounting
window dressing

A company's financial performance for a period is its **results**, which it **reports** in the form of a **profit and loss account**, indicating, unsurprisingly, whether it has made a profit or a loss. The equivalent document in the US is the **income statement**. A **pre-tax profit** or **loss** is one calculated before tax is taken into account.

results *162* ⇓

The accuracy of **accounts** such as the balance sheet and the profit and loss account is checked and supposedly guaranteed by **auditors**, outside **accountants** who specialize in this.

When a company's accounts are presented in a way that makes performance look better than it really is, the company may be accused of **window dressing** or **creative accounting**.

◆ **LANGUAGE NOTE**

Profit and loss and **window dressing** are also spelled with hyphens.

French Connection, owner of the fashion retailer of that name and of Nicole Farhi, the designer, has reported disastrous results for the year to end-January.

Gieves Group made a pre-tax loss of £105,000 in the 26 weeks to 31 July as a result of £250,000 costs incurred in the redundancy programme at Redwood.

redundancy *52* ⇑

Substance should triumph over form in situations of window-dressing and off-balance-sheet financing. It is argued that assets and liabilities should be brought together on the balance sheet if this is necessary to give a true and fair view, whether or not the information involved is specifically required by legislation.

If companies are so defensive and embarrassed about creative accounting, now is the time for auditors to toughen up and insist that as much of it as possible is stripped out of reported figures.

Mr Tweedie says: 'We looked at the three basic elements in accounts: sources and application of funds, the profit and loss account and the balance sheet and decided that they all had to change. We tore up the profit and loss account.' A completely new cash flow account, which identifies inflows and outflows previously hidden, was introduced.

The income statement shows the amount that the company earned during the year. After deducting the costs of goods sold and other expenses, International Paper had total earnings before interest and taxes of $1610 million.

earnings *162* ⇓

12 **Furious window dressing.** Read this article from the *Sunday Times* about the publication of a book called *Accounting for Growth* and answer the questions.

REVEALED: HOW TOP FIRMS MASSAGE THEIR PROFITS

Details of how some of Britain's biggest companies are using questionable techniques to inflate their reported profits and give a misleading impression of their true financial position are revealed today. They are contained in an exclusive extract of *Accounting for Growth*, the controversial book by Terry Smith, a banking analyst at UBS, Phillips and Drew, which has caused a storm in the City. ...

The three biggest accounting offenders identified in the book are: Grand Metropolitan, the leisure and drinks group; Ladbroke, the hotels and gambling firm; and Trafalgar House, the construction and leisure conglomerate.

According to Smith, Grandmet uses nine of 12 questionable, but legal, accounting techniques. Ladbroke and Trafalgar use eight each. Five more firms use seven: British Aerospace, the defence conglomerate; Granada, the television company; Rank Organisation, the leisure group; Ratners, the jeweller; and Albert Fisher, the food distributor. Forty-four companies are identified as using five or more of the techniques, which Smith describes as 'financial engineering'. They include firms from almost every sector, but most are in hotels and leisure, stores, media, brewing and distilling and food manufacturing.

1 If you inflate a figure, you e x a _ _ _ _ _ _ a t e it.

City 148 ⇓

2 Are offenders necessarily criminals?

conglomerate 11 ⇑

3 If something is questionable, some consider it d i s _ _ _ _ _ _ t.

4 Does 'financial engineering' show approval?

sector 6 ⇑

In the book, Smith claims his study provides 'an amazingly accurate guide to the companies to avoid'. He says reported profits are a poor guide to the underlying health of a company because they are 'the result of the accountant's "true and fair view", or to give a more polite name, a guess'.

According to Smith, 'much of the apparent growth in profits that occurred in the 1980s was the result of creative accounting rather than genuine economic growth'.

He advises investors to read companies' annual reports from back to front, ignoring the chairman's statement and the directors' report, which he describes as a 'gloss'. ...

5 Who should 'avoid' these companies?

6 Is the underlying state of something easy to see?

7 If something is apparent, is it always real?

8 If you put a gloss on a bad situation, you try to pretend things are better than they really are. What is the bad situation referred to here?

The bottom line

bottom line

The **bottom line** is an informal way of talking about the results of a company: the so-called bottom line of the profit and loss account. The bottom line also means the final result or the most important aspect of something.

Consolidated sales for Nissan and 100 subsidiaries worldwide dropped by 3.4 per cent to 6,198 billion yen (£37.1 billion). But the bottom line performance was that a profit of 85.7 billion yen (£513 million) last year turned into a 108 billion yen loss.

But the bottom line was unmistakable: build cars on time, of quality, or we don't want them.

13 Flowing through to the bottom line. Match the two parts of these sentences.

1 Investors in People is being promoted as the way to create a training culture among British businesses and manufacturers.
2 At the Annual General Meeting of the Pearson Group, the chairman Lord Blakenham felt confident enough to tell shareholders that
3 Airline managers understand that, however bad their bottom line might look,
4 Besides adding to its bottom line,
5 His strength is to assess what is happening and then to go straight to the bottom line.
6 Del Giudice's biggest enemy within the Rank Organisation was John Davis,
7 I do a couple of applications and three or four speculative letters every week.

a a brilliant if ruthless accountant whose only concern was the bottom line.
b I get nice replies, but the bottom line is there's no work.
c It aims to improve performance and have a direct impact on the bottom line of company results by helping employers to reach a high, nationally recognised standard of training and development for all their workforce.
d the overall performance of the group is improving and that even where sales are flat, cost cutting is starting to come through to the bottom line.
e their fleets must be continually updated if they are to attract passengers in an increasingly competitive market.
f This concern for the bottom line led Stevens earlier this year to close *Punch*, a magazine that was losing £2 million a year.
g Apple hopes its new portable will enhance its reputation as a leader in bringing new computing technologies to market.

Lame ducks and company doctors

sick
ailing

Companies in financial difficulty are often described as **sick**, or **ailing**, a word used more in this context than to describe people who are ill.

bleeding
haemorrhaging
red ink

Commentators talk about companies in difficulty in terms of **bleeding** or **haemorrhaging red ink** (from the days when negative figures were written in red ink in company accounts).

lame duck

Companies in trouble and needing outside help are also often referred to as **lame ducks**, likening them to birds with difficulty in walking.

◆ **LANGUAGE NOTE**

Haemorrhaging is spelled **hemorrhaging** in American English.

At a recent count, India had more than 250,000 'sick enterprises'. Officially, they are forbidden to close. They are expected to go on making losses for ever at taxpayers' expense.

By 1990, the company was ailing and Marc Bohan, formerly designer at Christian Dior, was brought in to revive its fortunes. He attracted new customers but not enough to save the company.

After more than a decade of protection, Ford, General Motors and Goodyear were still bleeding red ink.

Since Mr Dixson became chief executive on September 1 last year his main priority has been to drive down debt through a programme of tighter controls and disposals. Shining through the flood of red ink in the 1993 results were two signs of hope. Debt had been reduced from £148 million when Mr Dixson took over to £117.8 million at the year end and the cash haemorrhage had been staunched, mainly by getting working capital down.

disposal 21 ⇑

The manufacturing methods of Rover, once the lame duck of British industry, have been transformed thanks to that company's partnership with Honda.

company doctor

turn round

turnaround
turnround

Sometimes **company doctors**, people who specialize in this area, are brought in to **turn round** companies in difficulty and make them successful again. If they succeed in difficult circumstances, the resulting **turnround** or **turnaround** is often described as dramatic or remarkable.

Dan-Air does not have immediate cash problems after the latest holiday season, but that will start to change by the end of next month, when borrowings will start to mount again. David James, the company doctor trying to turn Dan-Air round, approached a substantial group of its shareholders last week with an outline request for fresh funds.

shareholder 9 ⇑

Despite the recession, the specialist engineering company has completed a remarkable turnround, moving from losses into profit and assembling a portfolio of businesses with growth potential.

recession 178 ⇓

14 Troubleshooting specialist. Read this article from the *Financial Times* and answer the questions.

1 Are enfants terribles children?

2 Are opinionated people outspoken?

3 Is someone's forte something that they are good at?

THE FLAMBOYANT TROUBLESHOOTER

Jean-Marie Descarpentries is an *enfant terrible* among French managers. Unusually flamboyant, voluble and opinionated, his reputation as a turnround specialist is laced with controversy.

His special talent is for provoking change in companies in crisis; managing in untroubled times is not his forte. 'Creative confusion' typically describes his style. He is fond of boasting that he has been fired from every job he has held with the exception of McKinsey & Co, the management consultancy, where he worked between 1969 and 1976.

The companies with which he has been involved include the glassmakers Saint Gobain of France and Glaverbel of Belgium. As chairman and chief executive of Carnaud, a leading French packaging group, he first restored the company to health, then led the £780 million acquisition of the UK's Metal Box Packaging in 1988.

What Descarpentries did for Carnaud has been described as a textbook corporate turnround. It lost Ffr159 million (£19.3 million) on sales of Ffr4.6 billion in 1981; by the time of the merger it was making Ffr365 million on sales of Ffr7.23 billion.

The merged company, one of Europe's largest in the packaging business, proved less of a success as Descarpentries found that his cerebral theories about managers who behave either as horsemen or monks drew little response from the pragmatic British. Tensions grew within the company, senior managers left and performance fell away. Finally, after two years of increasing tension he quit. Critics say he underestimated how hard it would be to restructure Metal Box.

Trained at the Ecole Polytechnique, he was a paratrooper while in the army. Stories abound of the tactics he uses to shock people into action. While he may have mellowed, he shows no signs of slowing down. At 57, he works extraordinary hours. Meetings often last until 10 or 11pm, explained only partly by the fact that during the week he lives by himself, joining his wife at the weekends at their 17th-century farmhouse south of Paris. For the average company doctor, Groupe Bull might be the last big turnround, but Descarpentries is already talking intriguingly about his next job.

4 If you boast about something, are you proud of it?

acquisition
12 ⇑

5 If you describe something as textbook, is it orthodox?

merger
19 ⇑

6 Would you like your boss to talk about managers as horsemen and monks?

7 If performance falls away, it d e t _ _ _ _ _ _ a t e s .

8 If stories abound, are there a lot of them?

9 If someone mellows, do they become
a) more extreme, or
b) less extreme in their behaviour?

10 If someone talks intriguingly about something, is it always clear what they mean?

Going bust

bankruptcy
file for bankruptcy

collapse

bankrupt

go bankrupt
go out of business

Unsuccessful companies may **collapse**, **go out of business**, or **go bankrupt**. **Bankruptcy** is the situation of going or being bankrupt. In America, companies in difficulty may declare their bankruptcy to the authorities or **file for bankruptcy** to get temporary protection from their creditors.

A company or an individual with debts that they are unable to pay may be declared a **bankrupt** by a court of law.

◆ **LANGUAGE NOTE**

Collapse is also used as a noun.

Airlines throughout the globe are losing money heavily and many are facing bankruptcy, takeovers and collapse.

As Japan's 'bubble' economy bursts, so thousands of companies are collapsing with it. Some 5,600 companies went bankrupt during the first seven months of this year.

In 1978 America's federal bankruptcy code was rewritten in order to make it easier to file for bankruptcy, to re-organise under Chapter 11 of the code, and then to re-emerge as a going concern even under the same management. That in effect reduced directors' worries about bankruptcy, pushing them to borrow more.

Towns in upstate New York are competing for new prisons – they provide jobs and it's an industry that's not likely to go out of business.

A bankrupt cannot be a director of a company and cannot start a new firm without informing customers and suppliers that he is bankrupt.

15 **Humble record-breaker.** Read this article from *The Times* and answer the questions.

THE HUMBLING OF BANKRUPT KEVIN MAXWELL

The humbling of bankrupt Kevin Maxwell, the youngest son of the late newspaper tycoon Robert Maxwell, will affect his business career, any aspirations he might have to hold public office and almost every detail of his financial affairs.

He faces an array of restrictions that amount to wearing a badge on which his

1 Aspirations are h _ _ _ _ s and amb _ _ _ _ _ _ s.

2 An array is a r _ _ _ _ e.

humiliating status is declared to the world. He is barred from becoming the director of a company or from being involved with the management of a company without the permission of the court. He cannot carry on a trade or business unless he uses the same name as that in which he was declared bankrupt. He cannot take any public office or become a magistrate. He can borrow up to only £250 as a private citizen. To obtain any large sum on credit he has to tell the creditor that he is an undischarged bankrupt. ...

The Official Receiver takes control of all the bankrupt's property, apart from basic necessities and the tools of his trade. In most cases the bankrupt can expect to be discharged from bankruptcy within three years, although he can apply for a discharge at an earlier date if, for example, he has paid off a substantial part of his liabilities.

Most of the trappings of the high life once enjoyed by Mr Maxwell have already gone. At the end of last year his global assets were frozen and a judge limited his living expenses to £1,500 a week. Mr Maxwell and his wife Pandora sold their eight-bedroom Georgian mansion in Chelsea, said to be worth £1.7 million. Mr Maxwell has now entered the history books as Britain's biggest bankrupt. ...

3 If you are barred from doing something, are you forbidden to do it?

4 Are creditors likely to lend money to bankrupts?

5 If you are a discharged bankrupt, are you still officially considered to be a bankrupt?

6 Are trappings the same as traps?

7 If your assets are frozen, are you allowed to sell them?

Salvaging the wreckage

crash
fold
go bust
go under
go to the wall

shake-out

More informal expressions for going out of business include **crash**, **fold**, **go bust**, **go under**, and **go to the wall**.

When a lot of businesses in an industry go bust at the same time, commentators talk about a **shake-out** eliminating these weaker companies.

◆ **LANGUAGE NOTE**

Shake-out is also spelled **shakeout**, especially in American English.

Small businesses in Britain are currently going bust at a rate of one every six minutes. After the 47,000 firms that went bankrupt last year, a further 80,000 are expected to go to the wall this year.

Instead of allowing them to collapse, triggering a chain reaction – remember one small company going under can bring down up to a dozen in its wake – the government should extend a lifeline.

John Bloom, whose washing machine company folded owing £2.5 million in 1964, has experimented with restaurants in Los Angeles, media road shows across the United States and hair tonic.

Disgraced American car manufacturer John de Lorean has been forced to sell his luxury New York penthouse home to pay a £5 million British tax debt. De Lorean, 66, whose Belfast car company crashed ten years ago with the loss of more than 2,000 jobs after receiving more than £77 million of taxpayers' cash, sent the money to receivers Cork Gully in London.

The Civil Aviation Authority licenses around 650 tour operators and yet the top 40 provide 83 per cent of all holidays on offer. This leaves the remaining 600 to fight for just 17 per cent of the market. A shake-out of the industry does seem to be likely later this year.

salvage

wreck
wreckage

Sometimes the image of corporate **wreckage** is used: the state of the company is likened to a car or plane after a serious accident. Commentators talk about trying to **salvage** something from the **wreck** or wreckage in the same way that shipwrecks are salvaged for anything of value that remains.

Some of PanAm's creditors, including Boeing and General Electric, were also creditors of Eastern. They had pleaded with the bankruptcy judge to close down Eastern last autumn, but instead he allowed it to remain airborne and continue to run down its cash resources. There is now little left for creditors to salvage from Eastern's wreckage. These creditors will be determined not to let the same thing happen to PanAm.

insolvency
receivers call in the receivers receivership
administration administrator
liquidation go into liquidation in liquidation liquidator
wind up a company cease trading

A company in a state of **insolvency** is unable to pay its debts.

Receivers are specialised accountants who are appointed, or **called in**, perhaps to find someone to **rescue** the company. Companies in this situation are in **receivership**.

In some circumstances, an insolvent company may be in **administration**, and the receivers may be referred to as **administrators**: see the exercise below.

If a company cannot be rescued, it is **wound up**, with the receivers or administrators selling what they can to pay off the debts. A company in this situation **goes into liquidation** and is then **in liquidation**. The receivers or administrators are in this case **liquidators** of the company.

An insolvent company that does not continue in some form **ceases trading**.

The magazine 'City Limits' was bought last summer by the publisher Terry Hornett from Clark Productions, which rescued it from receivership in 1990.

Valere Tjolle, who left thousands of holidaymakers stranded when his firm Land Travel crashed, has gone bankrupt. Land Travel called in receivers three weeks ago, leaving debts of more than £10 million, which are unlikely to be recovered. Grant Thornton, the liquidator, has listed 22,000 named creditors, and yesterday said Mr Tjolle, 47, had filed for personal bankruptcy.

In the US, a trustee is like a British receiver, except that he is there to get the company going again, not to wind it up.

Administrators found that an immediate liquidation of Polly Peck would have produced a deficit for shareholders of £384 million.

The banks had no alternative. If they had pulled the plug, Canary Wharf would have gone into liquidation and been sold off to the highest bidder and they would all have lost millions.

The accountant, David Adams of Cooper's & Lybrand, was shot while leaving Polly Peck's Istanbul offices in August. He was, apparently, mistaken for Chris Howell, one of the executives handling the administration of the now bankrupt fruits-to-electronics conglomerate. The gunman later claimed he was offered £5,000 for the shooting.

Six out of every 10 new businesses cease trading within their first ten years.

16 **Success in failure?** Read this article from *Today* and carry out the tasks.

Find:

a a word referring to insolvent companies as dead bodies and a word referring to insolvency experts as the people who deal with them.

b two expressions referring to insolvent companies in terms of an accident or explosion.

c a word referring to management consultancy profits in terms of gains to be made from war.

d an expression referring to what banks do to failing companies when they are no longer prepared to support them.

e a word referring to a period when weak companies go out of business when conditions get difficult.

f an expression that means 'short of cash'.

GOING BUST MEANS BOOM TIME FOR INSOLVENCY MEN

The insolvency experts, the undertakers who bury Britain's company corpses, are laughing all the way to the bank. They have enjoyed one of their best years in memory sweeping up the financial debris left by the recession, and senior partners of the biggest firms have become seriously rich. The top men have picked up over £1 million each, even before any division of partnership spoils. At the height of the shake-out two months ago, some 400 companies were plunging into receivership every month, triggered either by cash-strapped creditors or big banks pulling the rug. A 33% rise in insolvency work helped push up fee income at Touche Ross by 16% to nearly £350 million last year. Rival Arthur Andersen saw UK fee income jump 23% to over £330 million and Price Waterhouse has unveiled a 6% growth to over £400 million, with insolvency income boosted by no less than 40%. Another of the insolvency giants, Ernst & Young, who will be responsible for salvaging the wreckage of the failed Canary Wharf project, have enjoyed a 7% jump to nearly £400 million. All said hard times 'had bred a surge in demand for management consultancy'. Top partners such as Michael Jordan of Coopers & Lybrand can earn a staggering £400 an hour, equivalent to £3,200 a day or over £1 million a year. It is hardly surprising, then, that major crashes like BCCI, Brent Walker and Maxwell made a fortune for Touche Ross.

Crossword

Across

3 See 12 (5)
7 Insolvent companies ________ trading (5)
9 The profit and loss ________ is where the results are (7)
10 This, like invoice, can be a verb (4)
11 Debts are these (11)
12, 3. These are unlikely ever to be paid (3, 5)
13 Companies with a lot of debt in relation to equity are highly ________ (9)
15 Negative result (4)
17 You can't touch these assets, but they're there (10)
18 ________-term debts are repaid quickly (5)
19 A form of liability (7)
20 Amount sold, by value or quantity (5,6)

Down

1 Companies that finance themselves out of their own profits are this (4-9)
2 Something with value or earning power (5)
4 This type of inventive accounting may be legal, but is not always approved of (8)
5 What you try to do with the wreckage (7)
6 You hope that these do not become 12 across (11)
8 A company goes out of this when it ceases trading (8)
13 An overdraft is a form of ________ (4)
14 These costs change with the level of production (8)
16 Sales revenue may come in this watery form (6)

6 Towards the feelgood factor

Raising finance

raise capital raise finance stock market stock exchange bourse shares listed quoted

Companies needing money for development may **raise finance** or **raise capital** on the **stock market** or **stock exchange** by selling **shares**: investment certificates that vary in value, depending partly on company performance.

Company shares are **listed** or **quoted** on the stock market.

Stock markets may also be referred to as **bourses**.

◆ **LANGUAGE NOTE**

Stock market is also spelled as one word.

Businesses large and small need a capital market in which they can raise finance at the lowest possible cost.

US companies can't raise capital in Japan unless they are listed on the Tokyo Stock Exchange.

IKEA, despite an estimated annual turnover of £2 billion, is still private and is not quoted on any stock market.

turnover 114 ⇑

Most of the shares listed in New York are still domestically-based firms, but the shares of foreign companies account, on average, for a third of the shares listed on the main European bourses.

1 **Bourses of the world.** Put the sections of this book review from *The Economist* about *Chasing Mammon* by Douglas Kennedy into a logical order. (Mammon is the god of materialism; a crap shoot is an American game of chance played with dice. The first paragraph is a and the last f.)

TOURING THE BOURSES

a ...Douglas Kennedy writes about well-trodden places, New York, London, Casablanca, Singapore, Sydney and Budapest, but gives them a lift by looking at them through the eyes of the money-makers. At the start of his round of the people in half a dozen stockmarkets, he says he wanted to find out how the marketplace 'illuminated attitudes to money'.

b A good account of the new London is given in Mr Kennedy's story of a 'street kid' who got a humble job in the City and rose in the affluent 1980s to be a commodities trader making £300,000 a year.

c But there is no mystery why people want money. They just want it. Fortunately, Mr Kennedy declines to indulge in any dodgy philosophy.

d If his stories have any general message, it is that chance is important in getting rich. It is no wonder that quite sensible brokers consult astrologers. Mr Kennedy quotes one who says that playing the markets is a 'crap shoot' and astrology shortens the odds.

e None of this high-risk anxiety informs the bourse in Casablanca. Business lasts just 30 minutes each day, and that includes chat. Old hands in the City can recall when life there was as relaxed: starting work at mid-morning, a long lunch and home to Virginia Water before the rush hour.

f He had a high-spending wife, and lost everything except his sense of the ridiculous. ...

Financial centres

financial centre
City
Square Mile
Wall Street
trade
securities
bonds
commodities
currencies
foreign exchange
forex

Stock exchanges are found in **financial centres**. New York's financial centre is, of course, **Wall Street** and London's is the **City**, also referred to as the **Square Mile**.

Things **traded** in financial centres include:

securities: shares and **bonds**, investment certificates with a fixed rate of interest

commodities such as cereals and precious metals

currencies such as dollars, pounds, and francs on the **foreign exchange** or **forex** markets.

'Look at the value of the dollar. ... I'm glad now, I didn't take it with me.'

◆ **LANGUAGE NOTE**

Centre is spelled **center** in American English.

LBS researchers believe deregulation and technological advance will add to the concentration of the three main financial centres: London, New York and Tokyo.

Splits appeared yesterday in the ranks of leading City figures over crucial aspects of how to supervise and regulate the Square Mile.

A good start to trading on Wall Street lifted the London market later in the day.

Shares must compete with bonds yielding 6.8%.

President William Terry said the company's existing cash, marketable securities and anticipated revenue 'should be sufficient to satisfy cash needs for the current level of operations'.

revenue *114* ⥣

Currencies, commodities, government and corporate bonds: all are now issued and traded round the clock and round the world.

More money churns around in the forex markets than in any other: some $900 billion a day.

stock
stocks
equities

blue chip shares
blue chip stocks
blue chips

Shares are also called **stock**, **stocks**, or **equities**.

Blue chip shares, blue chip stocks, or **blue chips** are the safest share investments in leading companies.

stocks *74* ⥣

◆ **LANGUAGE NOTE**

Blue chip is also spelled with a hyphen.

Is now the time to buy equities?

'If your company's stock value shows a decline, you become a good target for takeovers, so management has to always do whatever it can to keep the value of the stock up,' he says.

takeover *12* ⥣

Among blue-chip stocks, General Electric climbed 1⅜ to 57¼, General Motors rose ⅝ to 49⅛, American Express added 1 to 36⅞, Westinghouse Electric gained 1¼ to 68⅜ and United Technologies added 1 to 55⅞.

Blue chips like ICI, Guinness, Reckitt & Colman and RTZ saw double-figure gains.

2 **Does it matter where you are?** Read this article from *The Economist* and answer the questions.

WHY LONDON?

How secure is London's role as a Financial Centre?

He's merchant-bank Bertie, who sets off at 6.30, and a dapper, well-heeled fellow he is, to be sure. Yet he crowds, with thousands of others, into a shabby train or bus headed for the City of London. They will all swarm through damp, grimy streets to their skyscrapers to do what? To cluster in some of the world's most expensive office space, to stare at flickering screens and pore over pages of numbers, and to talk on the telephone to other disembodied voices about this deal and that price.

Bertie's business has its ups and downs, but why does he do it in London? Much the same can be asked about New York and Tokyo, the other financial centres, now that computers, satellites and an end to capital controls have made money mobile. Yet only London is worrying about its future as a financial capital. ...

London is right to worry. Of the three main financial centres, its position is the most fragile. In New York and Tokyo a small amount of international finance is perched on a vast domestic market. In London, it is the other way around. The businesses it attracted in the past 30 years could as easily be done in New York, Tokyo or elsewhere.

In five short years, Tokyo has managed to wrest leadership of international bank-lending away from London. And then there is continental Europe, where Paris and Frankfurt are on the up. For the first time in centuries, London has rivals in continental Europe.

1 Are the main customers of merchant banks private individuals?

2 Dapper, well-heeled people are well-d _ _ _ _ _ _ e d and well-o _ _ .

3 Does the writer show approval of how people such as Bertie work?

4 If something such as a business has its ups and downs, is it, on the whole, OK?

5 London's position is the least s e c _ _ _ .

6 If you wrest leadership from someone, you _ _ _ _ it from them.

7 Rivals are c o m p _ _ _ _ _ _ _ .

Its easiest defence starts with the earth's rotation. Yes, some international business might revert to America or Japan, but until the world's Berties give up both sleep and dinner, there will be trading and other deals in the European time zone. For that business, London's rivals are still far behind. But this begs another question. Why have a centre at all?

Communication is now cheap and reliable, making it easy to trade, borrow and invest from the warmth of southern France or the cheapness of Glasgow. Businesses in which people have to see the whites of each other's eyes – such as mergers advice – might have to stay in finances inner cities. Others do not. ...

8 Why is the earth's rotation important?

9 'International business might revert to America or Japan' means that it might
a) go there, or
b) return there?

10 If a statement begs a question, has the question already been answered?

11 Why do people need to see the whites of each other's eyes when discussing mergers?

merger 19 ⇑

Market players

brokers
dealers
traders

investor
speculator

market makers
securities houses

market players

Traders, **dealers**, and **brokers** buy and sell on behalf of **investors**, traditionally seen as looking for long-term gains, and **speculators**, traditionally seen as looking for short-term ones.

Market makers are wholesalers of shares who keep supplies of the shares in which they deal, making a continuous market for buyers and sellers.

wholesaler 101 ⇑

Securities houses are large financial institutions offering a number of investment services.

People and institutions involved in a financial market are, informally, **market players**.

◆ **LANGUAGE NOTE**

Market makers is also spelt with a hyphen.

Some traders say the bond market was carried up by foreign investors and speculators, especially in Japan.

Dealers said the shares had got too far ahead of events, code for being overpriced.

The decline was slowed by the absence of many market players because of summer vacations.

Brokers in London reported heavy turnover in BP shares this week, usually towards the close of trading, when dealings on Wall Street are beginning. Several leading American securities houses have been buying shares this week, including Lehman Brothers and Salomon Brothers.

What market makers provide is immediacy, a very valuable service.

3 **Market players.** Match the two parts of these extracts.

1 According to City brokers, the results were better than expected. One leading market player said last night:

2 With Packer's private interests now thought to be well in excess of £1 billion,

3 Trading on little specific information,

4 But some market players still think earthquake speculation could have more impact on the oil markets.

5 There was a series of steps to soften big stock drops by interrupting trading

6 Investments in gold and dollars have risen sharply since mid-September

7 Sensible stock market players buy for the long term,

a the shrewd stock market player has spent more than A$250 million to take a 10 per cent stake in the troubled bank just as it appears to have hit rock bottom.

stake 9 ⇑

b 'The question is,' said Mr Barakat, 'was there any structural damage to the pipelines or anything else?'

c 'The underlying profitability is very strong. The share price fell because it has been so strong over the last few weeks.'

d because of market players' growing fears that the new cruzado is losing its value.

e especially small investors who can lose most of their profit in dealing costs if they buy and sell too often.

f market players in Tokyo began bidding up oil prices.

g to give market players time to pause and reconsider positions.

Share issues

share issue
share flotation
share offering

float

When companies raise finance by selling shares they make **share issues**, **share flotations**, or **share offerings**.

Companies making share issues and listed for the first time are **floated** on the stock market.

As Britain recovers from recession, companies will seek to raise finance through share issues. In the coming months, they will publish glossy prospectuses that celebrate their track records and invite people to part with their capital.

In New York on Friday, the group disclosed plans to issue $690 million through a global share offering. On top of the 40 million shares offered last December, the issue will dilute the holding of News Corp's chairman and chief executive, Rupert Murdoch, and his family, from around 46% to 33%.

holding 9 ⇑

Under one scheme being considered, the Post Office would be floated (have its shares sold) on the stock market in 1996. This would raise up to £5 billion for the government. Ministers are convinced that a flotation would be popular.

How do the venture capitalists regard the decline of the stock exchange's small companies sector? Public flotation is the traditional route for venture capitalists to realise gains and exit their investments.

venture capital 24 ⇑

rights issue
cash call

warrant

Companies looking for more finance may make a **rights issue** by offering new shares to existing shareholders at a discount. Rights issues are referred to informally by commentators as **cash calls.**

Buying **warrants** gives the right to buy a certain number of a company's shares for a given price at a later date. Warrants are similar to rights issues except that holders usually have longer in which to exercise their right to buy shares.

Construction group George Wimpey yesterday announced a £104 million rights issue, its first cash call since the company was floated on the stock market in 1963. Shareholders have been offered one new share, at 148p, for every four held. Wimpey shares fell 3p to close at 184p.

Salomon Brothers announced it will issue warrants on shares of Hong Kong Telecommunications Ltd. Under the offer, HK$62.5 million (US$8 million) of three year warrants will be issued in London, each giving buyers the right to one Hong Kong Telecommunications share at a price to be determined Friday. The 50 million warrants will be priced at HK$1.25 each, and are expected to carry a premium to the share price of about 26%. In trading on the Stock Exchange of Hong Kong, the shares closed Wednesday at HK$4.80 each. At this price, the shares will have to rise above HK$6.05 for subscribers to profitably convert their warrants.

4 Cash call crisis. Read this article from *The Times* and answer the questions.

MILLIONS WIPED OUT BY RIGHTS ISSUE BINGE

For punters who find the risk-rewards ratios of Las Vegas casinos a little too dull, the 1990s have turned up a more precarious pastime: investing in rights issues on the London stock market. The speed with which the funds from many of last year's cash calls have been wiped out

1 A binge is a period of e x c _ _ _ i v e consumption.
2 Punters is an informal word for people who bet money, in this case i n _ _ _ _ _ r s.
3 Are precarious pastimes risky?

would embarrass even the most stone-hearted croupier. Losing money is invariably painful; and the faster you lose it, the more excruciating it becomes. On that basis, several fund managers must feel that they have spent the past 18 months in a dentist's chair.

Last year was a record period for rights issues. About £9.2 billion pounds was raised by 143 companies. ... Much of that money has disappeared as Britain's economy has slid deeper into recession. With the exception of three leading food retailers Tesco, Argyll and Sainsbury and a handful of other companies, the recipients of the heaviest rights issues funds have all bombed.

Redland raised £280 million at 510p a share; its share price is now 333p. Amec £110 million at 200p a share (now 60p). Costain £77 million at 155p (24p). Taylor Woodrow £162 million at 200p (43p). ....

Sad stories every one, but at least they are still in business. Not so Mountleigh, which raised £96 million at 25p a share. The cash did not last even a year. Receivers moved in at the property group in May, leaving the shares high and dry at 3p. ...

4 Croupiers are officials at casinos who supervise roulette and other games. Are they famous for being kind-hearted?

5 Excruciating experiences are very p a _ _ _ _ _ l .

6 Most of these rights issues have bombed: they have failed badly. In British English, if something goes like a bomb, does it go badly?

retailer 101 ⇑

7 If something is left high and dry, is it in a good position?

Derivatives

derivatives

options
futures
swaps

More exotic financial products include **derivatives** such as:

options: certificates that give the right to buy specific securities at a given price up to a certain point in the future.

futures: a futures contract is a contract to buy something like a given quantity of a commodity or a certain number of securities for delivery at an agreed time in the future at a price agreed now.

swaps: for instance, a borrower agrees to exchange fixed interest payments on a loan with another borrower's variable interest payments, each borrower thus making the type of payments that suits them better. Another type of swap is described in the example.

Derivatives, which include futures, options and swaps, are special contracts whose value reflects movements in the price of underlying assets: equities, bonds, commodities.

An option gives its owner the right to buy or sell a specified amount of an underlying investment at a fixed price. Purchasers of 'call' options will profit only if the underlying investment moves up enough to cause the option's value to exceed its cost. Purchasers of 'put' options will profit only if the underlying investment has a major decline. Option buyers win so infrequently, says Alex Jacobson, an options specialist at the Chicago Board Options Exchange, because 'option buyers are betting on extraordinary events and they don't happen very often.'

A futures contract is an order that you place in advance to buy or sell an asset or commodity. The price is fixed when you place the order, but you don't pay for the asset until the delivery date. Futures markets have existed for a long time in commodities such as wheat, soybeans and copper. The major development of the 1970s occurred when the futures exchanges began to trade contracts on financial assets such as bonds, currencies and stock market indexes.

Suppose that the Possum company wishes to borrow deutschemarks to help finance its European operations. Since Possum is better known in the United States, the financial manager believes that the company can obtain better terms on a dollar loan than on a deutschemark loan. Therefore the company issues $10 million of 5-year 12 per cent notes in the United States. At the same time Possum arranges with a bank to swap its future dollar liabilty for deutschemarks. Under this arrangement the bank agrees to pay Possum sufficient dollars to service its dollar loan; in exchange, Possum agrees to make a series of annual payments in deutschemarks to the bank.

5 Critics of derivatives. Read this extract from the *Wall Street Journal* and answer the questions.

A DISTRACTING SIDESHOW?

... Mario Gabelli, a star of the investing world, says, 'My gut says the negatives of derivatives far outweigh the benefits.' Like others, Mr Gabelli says that if futures cause investors to lose confidence in stocks, they will move away from stocks – as many others have already done. And those who remain, he says, will demand a

1 'Gut' in this meaning is often used in the expression gut r _ _ _ _ _ _ n.

higher return and over the time raise the cost of capital to companies.

Essentially, the critics of stock index futures fall into two camps. One group says the futures contribute to stock market volatility; the other contends that futures are a sideshow of speculation that detracts from the stock market's basic function of raising capital.

'Before futures,' says New York investor Michael Harkins, 'you actually had to pay attention to whether the thing you were buying had any intrinsic value.' While it was once expected that futures would mimic stock prices, traders now routinely check the futures markets in Chicago before they buy or sell stocks. When Chicago jumps up or down, the New York Stock Exchange follows.

On Tuesday, for instance, the Dow Jones Industrial average plunged 80 points in little more than an hour. Then, in the space of a 20-minute coffee break, the average rallied almost all of the way back.

Paul Lesutis, who manages more than $3 billion of investments at Provident Capital Management Inc., blames the futures markets for leading the way. 'The fundamentals don't change in an hour,' he says. 'I think they should close down the futures exchange and then we could get back to investing.' ...

2 People will want a higher return on their __________.

3 Are volatile things predictable?

4 Is Harkins saying that stocks have intrinsic value, whereas futures don't?

5 If X mimics Y, does it copy it?

6 If the stock market rallies, does it:
a) continue to fall,
b) level off, or
c) rise after falling?

7 Are the fundamentals the 'real' underlying reasons for stock market behaving as it does?

Trading on the markets

trade
trading
- active trading
- moderate trading

change hands
turnover

Shares **change hands** when they are **traded**. When there is a lot of **trading** in a market, **turnover** is high.

Trading is most often described as **moderate** or **active**.

Trading volumes, too, have shot up; turnover is up tenfold from Friday's depressed levels.

New York: After an uncertain start, shares moved ahead in moderate trading.

About 5.4 million Jaguar shares changed hands in active trading on London's stock exchange Friday, and Jaguar shares moved up 19p to 696p.

dull
lacklustre
light
negligible
quiet
slow
sluggish
thin
weak

bumpy
choppy
erratic
hesitant
mixed
uncertain
volatile

brisk
heavy
hectic

frantic
frenetic
frenzied

Trading on the stock exchange and on other markets can also be:

a **dull, lacklustre, light, negligible, quiet, slow, sluggish, thin**, or **weak** when activity is low.

b **bumpy, choppy, erratic, hesitant, mixed, uncertain**, or **volatile** when the overall direction of prices is not clear.

c **brisk, heavy,** or **hectic** when there is a high volume of trading, in other words high turnover of shares.

d **frantic, frenetic**, or **frenzied** when there is a very high volume of trading.

◆ **LANGUAGE NOTE**

Lacklustre is spelled **lackluster** in American English.

6 **Dull or frenzied or something else?** Say to which of the above groups a–d the missing words in these extracts belong. (It's not always possible to say exactly which words are missing.)

1 After five or six weeks of ______________ trading and rapidly rising prices the black pepper market has entered a quieter period.

2 Analysts debated the meaning of sluggish trading volume. Optimists argued that ______________ trading volume signaled that investors remain confident. But pessimists countered that investors aren't being tempted into the markets at current price levels.

3 BASE METALS SOAR IN HECTIC TRADING AT LME. In one of the most ____________ days on the London Metal Exchange in living memory, prices soared yesterday as wave after wave of investment fund and speculative buying took copper, aluminium and lead to fresh four-year peaks and nickel and zinc to their highest levels for two years.

4 Foreign exchange dealers survived on adrenalin, coffee and sandwiches as currency markets entered a second day of ____________ trading. Wednesday was bad. Thursday, if anything, was worse.

5 ____________ trading on the Taiwan stock exchange yesterday pushed volume to a record $7.64 billion as optimistic small investors bought heavily and big investors took profits ahead of a possible change in tax rules.

6 PRECIOUS METALS. The ____________ trading pattern of prices continued, with gold and silver declining and platinum rising again.

7 Prices fell in extremely thin trading. The ____________ trading activity came ahead of several key economic reports due out this week.

8 Seoul ended lower in ____________ trading as investors, including institutions, stayed on the sidelines.

9 SHARE PRICES CLOSE EASIER IN UNCERTAIN TRADING. Share prices moved sharply in an ____________ trading session in London yesterday, as equally uncertain trends in bonds kept investors confused over the near term outlook for domestic securities markets.

10 The Mexican bolsa had a highly volatile session with ____________ trading until the market received the positive news of discussions between the US, Canada and the International Monetary Fund on an emergency credit line.

Bull markets and bear markets

bear market
bearish

bull market
bullish

rally
rebound
recover
regain ground
regain lost ground

recovery

gains
wipe out gains

When market prices are rising people talk about a **bull market**, and if they think prices will continue to rise, people are **bullish**.

When prices are falling people talk about a **bear market**, and if they think prices will continue to fall, they are **bearish**.

If prices rise after a period when they have been falling, they **rally, rebound, recover, regain ground**, or **regain lost ground** in a **rally** or **recovery**.

If prices fall to below the level they were before rising, earlier **gains** are **wiped out**.

'Ah, the pain of running with the bulls too long.'

On a clear day in a bull market, some investors can see stock prices rising forever.

Mr Schaeffer says the current 'extreme' bullish view of bond investors 'is likely to be as incorrect' as the pessimism earlier this year.

In a bear market, investment managers tend to put a larger proportion of their money into FT-SE stocks because of their perceived defensive qualities.

There is very little investor demand for gold bullion. Prices tend to rise only a little on bullish developments, and they fall more on bearish ones.

Then Wall Street suddenly rebounded to a gain on the day. 'Rally, rally, rally,' shouted Shearson's Andy Rosen. 'This is panic buying.'

The FT-SE Index, which has lost nearly 150 points since it peaked last month, regained some of its lost ground and sprang back through the crucial 2,600 level to close at 2,616.3, up 22.7 points.

Many building and construction stocks rallied, recovering some losses.

Shares staged a spectacular recovery yesterday and regained a lot of the ground lost in Thursday's bloodbath.

Deutsche Bank jumped 28.5 marks early in the session, pulling the broader market along. But profit-making soon wiped out these gains.

7 **Market logic.** Which word from this section is missing from all these extracts? What is its grammatical form in each case?

1	But remember that it took two years for the market to	....	from the mid-seventies crash,' Mr Seaman added.
2	the announcement of a rights issue, the shares	....	to just 4p down on the day at 129p, 19p higher than the
3	Glaxo chief executive. As soon as market sentiment	....	, the shares should bounce sharply.
4	foreign stock markets, led by the Japanese market, have	....	faster from the October 1987 crash than have the US
5	rate increase by the Bank of Japan. London shares	....	some lost ground, largely on technical factors as Chance
6	In London, Euro Disney shares closed down 5p at 845p,	....	from 828p. In Paris, the shares opened at FF86
7	on turnover 2% higher at £712 million. The	....	is largely due to a huge cost-cutting exercise. T&N cut

Insider dealing

insider dealing
insider trading

Chinese walls

Insider dealing or **insider trading** is the buying or selling of securities by people who have more knowledge than others of the company involved because they are connected with it in some way.

Financial institutions are supposed to take measures to prevent knowledge gained in one department from being used in other departments to trade in shares at an unfair advantage. These measures are informally known as **Chinese walls**.

'Your accountant won't be able to bail you out this time, Mr. Potter.'

The International Stock Exchange saw through its first insider dealing prosecution when two brothers pleaded guilty at Taunton Magistrates' Court yesterday. Peter and John Lukins sold shares in Pittard Garner in July shortly before the leather company warned of losses. The pair learned of Pittard's problems through a remark made after church one Sunday by Derek Foote, the company's group accountant. The Lukins saved about £5,000 through selling stock ahead of the collapse in Pittard's share price.

Imagine if a chap from a consultancy spends 18 months at the Trade and Industry Department and then goes back to the City. Can we really believe that Chinese walls will stop him using what he has learnt to help his other clients?

8 **Wrongdoing 1.** This article from *The Times* is about accusations of insider dealing in gilt-edged securities or gilts: British government bonds. Complete the article with the expressions listed. Each expression is used once.

a	Chinese walls	c	inside	e	dealers	g	complaints
b	trades	d	insider dealing	f	allegations	h	leak

LOAN LEAK RUMOUR SWEEPS MARKET

The Bank of England is believed to be looking into complaints that several banks this week traded on ___________ (1) information about the Government's £7.25 billion loan, announced on Thursday. Last night, National Westminster, one of the banks that arranged the loan, firmly denied there had been any ____________ (2) from its syndicated loan department or that it had made any unusual ____________ (3) in the gilt-edged market.

Martin Owen, chief executive of Natwest Markets said: 'We have had no complaints ourselves and no indication of any ____________ (4) from the Bank of England. Our syndicated lending happens behind ____________ (5), and we had no abnormal trading figures in the days before the loan. Claims like these happen when people are losing money and they love to say that someone else had preferential knowledge about an event.'

____________ (6) of ____________ (7) swept through the City all day, encouraged by gilt ____________ (8) and market makers who were caught out by the sharp rise in prices on Thursday afternoon, after the announcement of the government loan. ...

9 Wrongdoing 2. Match these types of wrongdoing to their definitions.

bribery
embezzlement
fake
forgery
forgeries
fraud
market rigging
money laundering
racket
scam

1 **bribery**	a Making or **faking** false documents, banknotes, or artworks. These are called **forgeries** or **fakes**.
2 **embezzlement**	b Illegally giving someone money so that they act in your favour
3 **forgery**	c Any illegal money-making activity.
4 **fraud** or **racket** or **scam**	d Fixing the price of something illegally.
5 **market rigging**	e Illegally taking money from the organization you work for.
6 **money laundering**	f Disguising the criminal origin of money such as drug money.

Unveiling results

results
announce results
report results
unveil results

earnings
distributed

dividend
yield
price/earnings ratio
P/E ratio

Stockmarkets eagerly await company **results.** A company's share price is obviously affected by these: whether it has made a profit or loss over a given period, and how much.

results 135 ⇑
profit 135 ⇑
loss 135 ⇑

Commentators talk about companies **announcing, reporting**, or **unveiling results.**

A part of profits or **earnings** for a given period may be **distributed** to shareholders in the form of a **dividend.**

A share's **yield** is the dividend expressed as a percentage of the share price.

The **price/earnings ratio**, or **P/E ratio**, of a company's shares is the earnings of the company per share expressed as a multiple of the share price.

Dixons, the UK's biggest electrical retailer, unveiled its results yesterday and they received a mixed reaction from the City.

Securicor announced results for the year to September showing a profit advance of 65 per cent to £54.5 million.

Cray Research Inc reported surprisingly weak results for the second quarter and indicated it expects significantly lower earnings for the year.

POOR EARNINGS OUTLOOK FORCES SEDGWICK TO HALVE DIVIDEND.

Mr Canelo suggests that investors compare price/earnings ratios (the price of a share divided by a company's per-share earnings for a 12-month period) with projected growth rates. 'If you think earnings will grow at 20% a year, it's all right to pay 20 times earnings,' he says. But don't pay 30 times earnings for a company that's expected to grow at 15% a year.

Wall Street is sharply divided over whether General Motors is a bargain in light of its 6% dividend yield, or an unnecessary risk at a time when the outlook for cars and the economy is uncertain.

ordinary shares
preference shares

common stock
preferred stock

When a company distributes earnings in the form of a dividend, holders of **preference shares** get priority over holders of **ordinary shares**. Likewise, if a company goes into liquidation, preference shareholders are paid off before ordinary shareholders.

liquidation 144 ⇑

Ordinary and preference shares are referred to in American English as **common stock** and **preferred stock**.

The group's cash flow has been boosted by its failure to pay dividends on any of its ordinary or preference shares since January. Ratner's paid a 2.4p interim dividend last year.

Farm and Home Financial Corp won't pay its third-quarter dividend on common stock as a result of the previously announced third-quarter loss.

Per-share earnings also shrank because of dividends on a new series of preferred stock.

10 **Piles of cash.** Read the examples and complete the commentary with the key words.

Key words	Commentary
equity share capital shareholders' funds reserves capital spending cash pile cash mountain sit on a cash pile sit on a cash mountain	Earnings not distributed are _ _ _ _ _ _ _ _ , which may be used to finance a company's development in _ _ _ _ _ _ _ _ _ _ _ _ _ _ _ in investment, or paid out in a later period to shareholders. A company with a lot of reserves is said to have, or _ _ _ _ _ , a _ _ _ _ _ _ _ _ or _ _ _ _ _ _ _ _ _ _ _ _ _ . Like **share capital** or **equity**, reserves are part of _ _ _ _ _ _ _ _ _ _ _ _ ' _ _ _ _ _ .

shares *9* ⇑

shareholder *9* ⇑

Company law forbids dividend payments if there is a deficiency of distributable reserves.

Ford poured more than $1.63 billion into automotive capital spending, or 55% more than in the last quarter. The capital spending helped eat into Ford's deep cash reserves.

Last year the group saw the value of its shareholders' funds soar, and a huge debt mountain of A$1.5 billion turn into a cash mountain of A$300 million.

debt *128* ⇑

It also sits on a big cash mountain, but even Toyota executives are now worried how much longer the recession is going to continue.

Dunhill was sitting on a cash pile of £179 million last year, a figure which has shrunk to £120 million due to spending in Europe on new stores and on promotion.

Return on shareholders' funds relates profit to the sum of share capital, reserves, and the profit and loss account balance.

profit and loss account *135* ⇑

Market movements 1

This section looks at key verbs used to talk about rising and falling share prices.

Going up

advance
climb
increase
rise
gain ground

These words are used to talk about prices going up. They do not in themselves indicate by how much the prices have gone up.

'I should warn you, Mr Dobbs, that share prices can go down as well as up.'

BAT industries climbed 11 pence to 888, and Pearson advanced 18 pence to 764.

SmithKline Beecham, a big British drugs firm, has just announced its third-quarter results. The price of its shares increased by 2.5% in London; on Wall Street by 6%.

Unilever's shares rose 12p to 1,080p after talks with analysts despite the fact that its ambitious global ice-cream and yoghurts plan was announced after hours.

Stores and consumer goods gained ground after the good inflation news and on hopes of interest rate cuts.

Going down

decline
drop
fall
head south
lose ground
retreat
slide

These words are used to talk about prices going down. They do not in themselves indicate by how much the prices have gone down.

Racal Electric, which traded 11 million shares, declined 12 to 218.

A predicted slowdown in the personal computer industry led to broad selling in a variety of technology shares. Compaq Computer dropped 2 to 88⅛ and Microsoft fell 3¼ to 52.

Barclays retreated 10p to 324p on further consideration of Thursday's worse than expected figures.

A slump in bank lending caused by sliding shares in Tokyo could feed quickly into other economies.

Shares lost ground again yesterday with the 100 constituent FT-SE share index closing 23 points down at 2,036.2.

Capital Holdings stock returns are not directly correlated with market returns. Sometimes Capital will head south while the market goes north, or vice versa.

Going up by small or moderate amounts

edge ahead
edge higher
edge up
firm

These words are used to talk about prices when they rise by a small or moderate amount.

◆ **LANGUAGE NOTE**

Edge cannot be used by itself in this context. It must be followed by **ahead**, **higher**, or **up**.

Amber Day's share price edged ahead 1p to 35p as news of Mr Green's departure outweighed the figures.

Chemicals were mixed, while oils edged higher.

Wall Street edged up 0.4% and London 0.2%.

National Semiconductor firmed ¼ to 7½ despite reporting a $21.9 million loss for its latest quarter, a larger loss than analysts generally expected.

Going up by large amounts

jump
leap
roar ahead
roar up
rocket
shoot ahead
shoot up
skyrocket
soar
surge (ahead)

These words are used to talk about prices when they rise by larger amounts, or when they increase quickly or sharply.

Forte's shares were among the week's best performers, jumping 20p to 309p.

Euro Disney shares leapt 40p to 790p on news that the chairman, Robert Fitzpatrick, would be handing over to Phillipe Bourgignon in April. Brokers argued that the Frenchman would do a better job in his own country than the American.

Shares in airports group BAA roared ahead 14p to 671p on news of a seven-year, £160 million contract with poster sites space seller Sky Sites.

Other auto makers also gained, Mazda Motors roaring up ¥33 to ¥621 and Isuzu Motors adding ¥16 at ¥517.

The FT-SE index rocketed 21.2 points to 2538.4 as dealers keyed in to a new mood of optimism.

The City expects year-end profits to top £1.5 billion. The shares shot ahead to 755p, a jump of 31p.

Sainsbury's share price has shot up relative to its sector, underlining its position as the ultimate defensive stock in times of trouble.

Turner Broadcasting is moving to act while the company is hot. Its Class A stock has skyrocketed in the past year, from a low of $7.50 a share to a close of $53.875 a share in trading Friday.

Pilkington shares soar on management buy-out speculation.

management buy-out *24* ⇑

While shares in foreign oil firms have been falling, shares in American oil and gas production companies have surged ahead.

Going down by small or moderate amounts

dip
drift (lower)
ease
edge down
edge lower
slip (lower)

These words are used to talk about prices when they fall by a small or moderate amount.

◆ **LANGUAGE NOTE**

Edge cannot be used by itself in this context. It must be followed by **lower** or **down**.

Guinness dipped another 11p to 478p and most food and drink stocks drifted lower.

ICI eased 11p to 1184p in spite of favourable assessments of the Zeneca subsidiary's new antibiotic product at a medical conference.

subsidiary *11* ⥣

Full-year profit edged down 8% to $60.8 million, or 76 cents a share, from $66.4 million, or 89 cents a share.

Stocks and bonds edged lower as trading activity remained sluggish.

Manders continued to lose ground, slipping another 10p to 188p, making a two-day fall of 23p, as shareholders with about one-third of the equity gave the 'thumbs-down' to the hostile offer from rival paint-maker Kalon.

Going down by large amounts

dive
nosedive
plunge
plummet
tumble

These words are used to talk about prices when they fall by large amounts.

◆ **LANGUAGE NOTE**

The past tense of **dive** is **dived** in British English and **dove** in American English.
Nosedive is also spelled with a hyphen.

Even before the resignations were announced, the index dove 32.5 points to close at 2129.4.

Shares of Hilton Hotels Corp., which has put itself up for sale, nosedived $21.50 to $85 a share.

Investors started a wave of frenetic share selling, sending the Hang Seng Index plunging 201 points. One broker said, 'It was as near panic as I've seen in 20 years.'

Last night Ratner flew home to save his struggling jewellery empire. In the past year, almost £500 million has been wiped off its market value and the shares continue to plummet.

Grand Met, the drinks and food group, tumbled 34p to 378p, after issuing a warning that pre-tax profits will be virtually in line with last year's £950 million.

Going down fast by very large amounts

collapse
crash
crumble
slump

These words are used to talk about prices if they fall by very large amounts, especially if they fall very quickly.

There seem to be few areas of the world where Brent's operations were not under pressure, and the news sent the group's share price crashing 30p lower to 99p.

Pittard's share price tumbled when the price of sheepskins collapsed.

Lonrho is limping towards its year-end, its shares battered by City disaffection, its profits ravaged by recession and the crumbling platinum price.

Southgate has seen Thorn's share price slump amid City concern that the weakening global music market meant it had paid too much for Virgin.

11 Rising and falling prices: verbs. Many of the same verbs can be used to talk about things other than share prices. Choose the correct alternative for each sentence.

1 The cost of living ____________ as high as 3.1% on a year-to-year basis in June.
slipped *climbed* *plummeted*

2 British operating profits ____________ from £51 million to £19.2 million last year.
edged down *tumbled* *skyrocketed*

3 Industrial output grew by 25.6% in 1992 over the previous year, as China's total economy ____________ by more than 12%.
slid *edged up* *shot ahead*

4 Lodz's rapid growth in the 19th century – between 1877 and 1914 the population ____________ from 50,000 to almost 500,000 – meant there was little town planning.
slumped *leapt* *nosedived*

5 Farm prices ____________ 0.7% from September as raw milk prices continued their rise.
edged up *rocketed* *surged*

6 Total car production ____________ 5% because of lower sales in the US, where all European car makers are struggling with weak demand.
shot ahead *slid* *increased*

7 A year ago, people selling their homes routinely received as many as six offers, with the winning bid often higher than the asking price. Prices ____________ as much as 35% in a single month last year.
edged up *skyrocketed* *firmed*

8 Japanese production has ____________, falling by 9% from its peak in 1991.
risen *edged down* *plummeted*

9 The dollar ____________ to its lowest level against the mark for 18 months.
slumped *rose* *advanced*

10 Sales held steady, but margins more than halved from 5.6 to 2.4%, and profits ____________ from £29.7 million to £12.1 million.
drifted lower *crumbled* *leapt*

Market movements 2

This section looks at key nouns used to talk about rising and falling share prices.

Going up

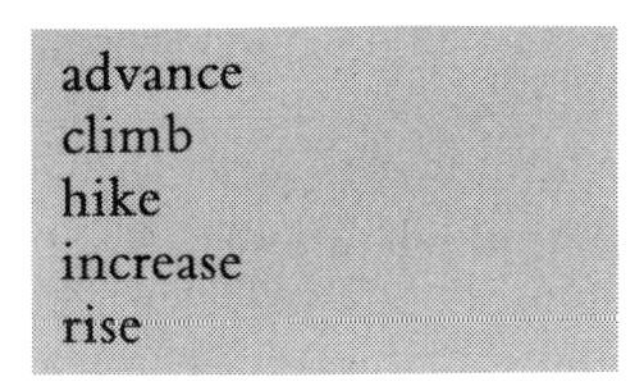

These words are used to talk about prices going up. They do not in themselves indicate by how much the prices have gone up.

A further rally in Euro Disney saw the shares touch 1575p, an advance of 20p.

British Aerospace is deemed suddenly to have turned the corner – a fact underlined this week by a sharp climb in the share price.

Nicoli insists that last week's good results and accompanying hike in the share price should prove to the sceptics that the company is already on track.

The share price may be such that it would be more sensible to achieve an increase in share price before an issue of shares.

Investors trade much more heavily after a rise in share prices.

Going down

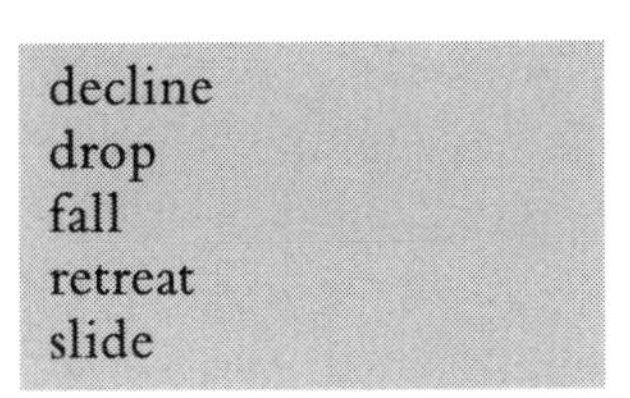

These words are used to talk about prices going down. They do not in themselves indicate by how much the prices have gone down.

The shares stayed at 205p despite the decline in the wider stock market.

Adobe plummeted $4.125 a share to close at $15.625, a drop of 40% from levels at the beginning of the month.

Howard Klein said the fall in the Airtours share price raises serious concerns as to the underlying value of the shares.

The index's peak was just 8 points off its all-time closing high of 2443.4. However, an outbreak of profit-taking, and a weak Wall Street opening, forced a retreat.

Kalon has the option of buying up to 10% of Manders in the market and may well do so after the slide in Manders' share price.

Going up by large amounts

These words are used to talk about prices when they rise by large amounts, or when they increase quickly or sharply.

A 22% profit rise took packaging group Boxmore to 187p, a jump of 10p.

Analysts are hoping that a revival in the economy will lead to a dramatic fall in provisions for bad and doubtful debts among the banks. Barclays led the way with a leap of 45p to 336p as 25 million shares changed hands.

The FT-SE 100 index of leading shares jumped 105.6 to close at 2,843.9. The surge, which added £21.7 billion to share values, was the biggest one-day rise since April 10, the day after the general election.

Going down by small or moderate amounts

These words are used to talk about prices when they fall by a small or moderate amount.

Analysts said the whole of the dip in the FT-SE 100 index of 1.7 points could be blamed on ICI's fall from favour.

Some analysts attribute the downward drift of bond prices to the continuing difficulty the market is having absorbing the glut of new supply.

A slip of 16 sent shares in Thorn EMI down to 972p.

Going down by large amounts

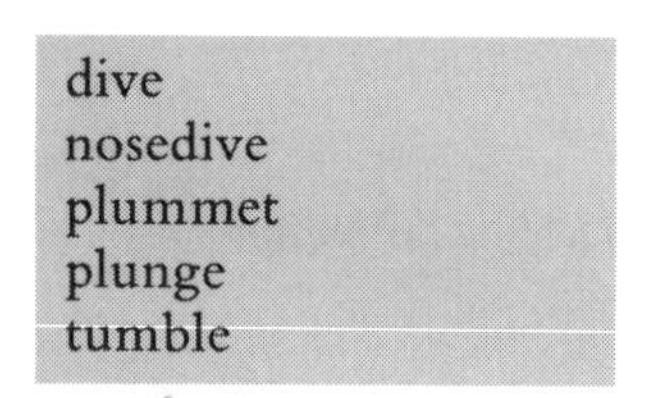

These words are used to talk about prices when they fall by large amounts.

◆ **LANGUAGE NOTE**

Nosedive is also spelled with a hyphen.

Pioneer's share price took a dive last month when rumours circulated that one of its subsidiaries was heading for bankruptcy.

The bank's share price promptly took a 50p nose-dive as astonished investors digested the results, which exceeded even the most pessimistic forecasts.

After reacting early in the trading day to Friday's plummet, prices firmed up again as traders took note of the stock market's partial recovery yesterday.

The plunge in Wellcome's share price on Friday was blamed by the company on an article in that morning's Wall Street Journal.

Several small technology concerns' shares took a tumble after the company disclosed poor earnings prospects.

Going down fast by very large amounts

crash collapse slump	These words are used to talk about prices if they fall by large amounts, especially if they fall very quickly.

Despite the crash in Japanese share prices last year, the Nikkei 225 has risen by 600% in dollar terms since the end of 1979, twice the gain of the world share-price index.

On the face of it, British Aerospace should be the bargain of the century. The collapse of its share price over the past two years has pushed the company's market value to just £471.8 million, down from a peak of more than £2 billion in 1989.

Results showed a £129 million pre-tax loss for the first half of 1992, with the regional aircraft business crashing £286 million into the red. They were met with a slump in the share price from 199p to 113p.

12 Rising and falling prices: nouns. Many of the same nouns can used to talk about things other than share prices. Choose the correct alternative for each sentence.

1 More people were pessimistic about the coming 12 months. The ____________ in confidence was most severe in Scotland.
advance *jump* *decline*

2 Dorling Kindersley lifted its annual profits to June by 105% to £7.5 million, with a 66% ____________ in turnover.
collapse *drift* *hike*

3 The dollar's ____________ to a fresh low of DM1.3860 failed to upset the market.
rise *dip* *surge*

4 Germany's industrial strength took a ____________ from second position in 1992 to 11th place now.
retreat *crash* *nose-dive*

5 Though the drop isn't enough to be called a slump, analysts said the hidden danger is that a small ____________ in steel consumption could trigger a nasty price war.
collapse *crash* *retreat*

6 Japan's production of cars, trucks and buses in September fell 4.1% from a year ago to 1,120,317 units because of a ____________ in exports.
plummet *slip* *nosedive*

7 Its money mountain has mushroomed from £217 million to £503 million, a massive ______________ of 132%.
drift *leap* *drop*

8 A dramatic 40% ______________ in steel prices has sent British Steel spiralling into the red.
rise *slump* *drift*

9 A ______________ in cold-drink sales during hot and sunny May and June helped Cadbury Schweppes push pre-tax profits ahead 13 per cent to £126 million.
fall *surge* *collapse*

10 Industrial output has stabilised, after falling 60% in 1991–2, the most precipitous economic ______________ in Eastern Europe.
drift *collapse* *dip*

Record highs and record lows

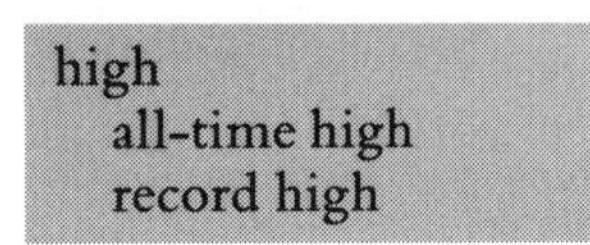
high
all-time high
record high

Records are broken: indices like the Dow Jones, Nikkei or FT-SE reach an **all-time** or **record high**.

Better economic news helped Wall Street gain 2.3%, hitting an all-time high. European bourses did well too. Frankfurt, Milan, Zurich and Stockholm all reached new highs for the year.

Tokyo share prices advanced broadly under the lead of Sony and other electrical issues, pushing the Nikkei to a record high in relatively active trading.

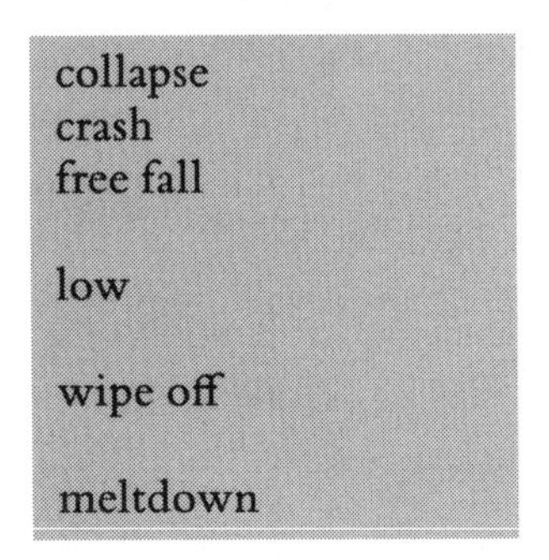
collapse
crash
free fall
low
wipe off
meltdown

But euphoria easily gives way to pessimism. When share prices fall a long way, commentators talk about billions of dollars, yen or whatever being **wiped off** share values. With prices falling to new lows, people may talk about a market **collapse** or **crash**.

If prices fall a very long way and there seems to be no limit to the amount they may drop, people use the parachuting image of **free fall**. Commentators may even compare events to a nuclear accident like Chernobyl and talk about a market **meltdown**.

Mr Granville says he wouldn't even think of buying until at least 600 to 700 stocks have hit 52-week lows; about 100 stocks hit new lows Friday. 'Most people,' he says, 'have no idea what a massacre pattern looks like.'

The leading FT-SE Index is now in free fall. A cool £15 billion has been wiped off share values in the last two days alone. The FT-SE closed last night well below 2,500 and I reckon it will plummet to 2,200 by April Fool's Day.

The Japanese authorities could contain a crash before it turned into a meltdown. But the risk is undeniably there.

13 **Massacre and meltdown.** The numbered extracts talk about falling share values in metaphorical terms. Relate the metaphorical areas a–h to the extracts and underline the metaphorical expressions. (One of the extracts contains two metaphors.)

a funerals	c air crashes	e fast-moving water	g earthquakes
b fires	d massacres	f torn material	h collapsed buildings

1 No insurance stocks escaped the bloodbath, but Sedgwick shares fell most heavily, losing 24 per cent of their value to close at 110p.

2 Lonrho boss Tiny Rowland, 74, saw his fortune in tatters again yesterday. The shares took a fresh nosedive, down 3p at 118p. A fall of 3p may not sound much, but to Lonrho's chief, holding a bumper 92 million shares, it was another nail in the coffin and cost him more than £2.7 million.

3 Sydney: Shares went into a tailspin, with the All-Ordinaries index losing 20.6 points at 1,354.7.

4 At their peak, the shares stood at 239p, so fingers have been burnt all the way down. Debts have piled up. Now we wait to hear if Burns Anderson is a totally burnt-out case, or whether there is hope of a phoenix-like recovery from the ashes of its former glory.

5 As ever, the collapse of a towering speculative market is exposing some ugly sights amid the rubble. Lots of share speculators have been charged with multi-billion-yen tax scams.

6 The giant was hoping to sell a minimum of 80 million shares worldwide but advisers could only find buyers for 50 million. This triggered a massive tremor on the stock market, already rocked by a shake-out on Wall Street and Tokyo.

7 A fresh tidal wave of selling engulfed the market yesterday and sent shares plunging to new lows for the year.

Key indicators

indicator
numbers
inflation
unemployment
jobless
growth
gross domestic product
GDP
gross national product
GNP

Stock markets may or may not react to **indicators** showing what is going on in the real economy, indicators such as:

unemployment: the number of jobless or people without work;

inflation: the rate at which prices are going up;

growth: the rate at which the value of economic output is expanding (or not). Output may be measured and expressed in terms of **gross domestic product (GDP)** or **gross national product (GNP)**. These measures vary slightly in their definitions, as the examples indicate.

output *68* ⇑

Indicators are also referred to as **numbers.**

'Stop worrying. Politicians always promise full employment, but I've yet to see one of them deliver.'

After the buoyant indicators seen in April, the May numbers could be less than dazzling.

The jobless rate in the UK has always been a lagging indicator, with the unemployment rate rising long after the upturn in the real economy has begun to take place.

In the long term, low inflation is the best path to steady growth.

The US Department of Commerce has just decided that it will concentrate more on GDP than GNP. GDP measures the value of all goods and services produced in America. GNP measures the total income of American residents, regardless of where it comes from; profits from a firm's overseas subsidiary as well as its earnings in America are included.

balance of payments

trade balance
trade deficit
trade figures
trade gap
trade surplus

import
export
- visible export
- invisible export
- invisibles

Another indicator is the **balance of payments**: these include the value of goods and services the country is **exporting** and **importing**. **Trade figures** show the **trade balance**.

Visible exports and imports are of physical goods. **Invisibles** are payments for services such as insurance and tourism.

If exports exceed imports there is a **trade surplus**. If not, there is a **trade deficit** or **trade gap**.

Current account figures also include transfers of money between countries, for example debt interest, or foreign workers sending money home.

Politicians and economists will have to wait six months for detailed information on Britain's trade position after publication of the December balance of payments figures on Thursday. Monthly trade figures for European Community imports and exports will not be published until mid-June while a new method of gathering information is introduced.

Take the trade deficit. Last year, the trade gap (including invisibles such as tourism and interest payments) represented nearly 4 per cent of our national income. This gap between what we produce and what we consume can only be financed by regular purchases of sterling by foreigners.

EXPORTS PUSH JAPANESE TRADE SURPLUS TO RECORD.

Tourism is the most important part of the Cypriot economy, contributing $154.9 million to the trade balance last year, three times as much as fruit and other visible exports.

August's £2.29 billion deficit in Britain's merchandise trade was offset slightly by a £300 million surplus in so-called invisible items, which include services, earnings from foreign investments and official transfers. The current account deficit reflects the merchandise trade deficit plus the invisibles surplus.

14 Diamonds are not forever. Read this article from *The Economist* and answer the questions.

AN ECONOMY'S BEST FRIEND

Measuring economic performance

Traditionally, governments have had four economic goals: strong growth, low inflation, low unemployment and a 'sound' balance-of-payments position. One rough and ready way to judge how an economy measures up to these goals is the 'diamond', invented by economists at the Organisation for Economic Co-operation and Development, the Paris-based club of rich nations.

The charts plot each of the four economic indicators (GDP growth, inflation, unemployment rate, and current account balance as a percentage of GDP) along one of the four axes, with the scales fixed so that the farther each plot is away from the origin, the better the country's performance. For each country, the four plots are joined up to form a diamond: the bigger the diamond, the better its record.

The charts compare the performance of the six biggest industrial economies in 1980-90 with the 'golden age' of 1967-73 before oil prices soared. In the 1960s and early 1970s, most economies scored relatively well on all four criteria. Japan and Germany boasted the biggest diamonds. But then came the oil shock: growth stalled, inflation and

1 What precious stones are traditionally a girl's best friend?

2 If something is sound, it is h_ _ _ _ _ y.

3 A plot on a graph is another word for a p_ _ _ t.

4 What is the singular of criteria?

5 If something stalls, does it slow down or stop?

unemployment rose. All countries saw their diamonds shrink dramatically during 1974-79, particularly Britain and Italy. The charts show that only two of these countries regained their sparkle during the 1980s.

Unemployment continued to rise everywhere. Only Japan and Germany bettered their inflation levels of 1967-73. This, along with bigger current-account surpluses, puffed up the size of their diamonds almost to the size they had been before the oil shock, although growth was slower for both countries, as it was for the other four countries as well.

The diamonds of the other four countries, however, all remained smaller in the 1980s than before 1974. America's shrank compared with the 1970s because of its huge current account deficit. Britain, France and Italy all had their diamonds badly dented on the left-hand side by higher unemployment. Shrinking from every direction, Italy's diamond looks in danger of disappearing.

6 If something shrinks, it gets s _ _ _ _ _ _ r .

7 If something regains its sparkle, does it become attractive again?

8 If X puffs up the size of Y, it makes it b _ _ _ _ _ r .

9 On which side of the diamond is the unemployment axis?

Boom and bust

boom
boom-bust cycle
business cycle

peak

downswing
downturn
turndown
turn down

slowdown
slow down

weaken

An economic **boom** with **booming** economic growth (increasing demand and production), inevitably **peaks**. Following this **peak** there is a **slowdown**, **turndown**, **downturn**, or **downswing** (periods of slower or negative growth), when the economy **slows down**, **turns down**, or **weakens**.

This pattern is the **business cycle**. In an economy where the pattern is extreme, it is referred to as the **boom-bust cycle**.

◆ **LANGUAGE NOTE**

The nouns **slowdown** and **turndown** are also spelled with a hyphen. **Business cycle** is also spelled with a hyphen.

'The business section feels warmer when the Dow Jones averages are up ..!'

Britain should not get carried away by all this boom-boom talk. The lesson of the last six years is that the boom-bust cycle is a recipe for economic disaster.

Now that Latin America is booming, it is difficult to remember how grim things were.

The National Bureau of Economic Research, America's official business-cycle watcher, uses a different yardstick: the monthly indicators for employment, industrial production, real business sales and real personal income. After whizzing these numbers through its computer, the NBER reckons the economy peaked in July last year.

Demand for goods from Britain's factories weakened in every region during the last four months.

Several components that track the health of the manufacturing sector of the economy turned down in September. These include new orders for manufactured consumer goods, delivery times and orders for new plant and equipment.

A consensus forecast is a handy way for businessmen to follow changing expectations, such as whether activity is slowing down or speeding up.

'Well... the signmaking business is booming...'

15 **Weakening nouns.** Match the two halves of these extracts containing nouns and -ing forms used to talk about weakening economies.

1 Mr Martin predicts that the trend rate of growth from the 1988 peak
2 Business people make several points to put the current slowdown in perspective.
3 Mr Heseltine accused Mr Brown of naivety in assessing Britain's economic problems
4 The report, showing slower economic growth
5 Demand for furniture has shrunk from a peak
6 With the slowing down of its rate of growth and its increasing relative backwardness,
7 We are no long talking about a normal downswing.

a and a severe weakening in the manufacturing sector, is a warning sign to investors.
b First, it is a downturn from an extraordinarily high level of activity.
c of £4.5 billion in 1989 to £4 billion last year.
d The dramatic changes show we have structural changes in Germany and the European Community.
e the USSR became too weak to sustain its role as a superpower.
f to 1999 will be no more than 1.75 per cent a year.
g while ignoring the world turndown.

Recession, stagflation, and depression

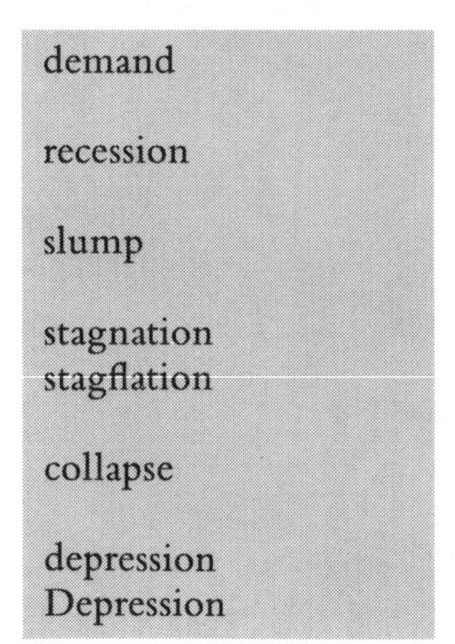

A slowdown in **demand**, the amount of goods and services that are bought, may be the first sign of a **recession**: a period with little growth, no growth, or even negative growth. A severe recession is a **slump**.

Stagflation is a combination of **stagnation**: low or negative growth, with high inflation and high unemployment.

When a recession is extremely severe and prolonged, commentators talk about economic **collapse** and **depression**. The **Depression**, with a capital D, usually refers to the years following the Wall Street crash of 1929.

It is now clear that the Germans and many other EC nations are desperately worried that the European recession could turn into a slump unless action is taken urgently.

There is still strong demand for champagne, but in a recession, it has to be sold at a price people can afford.

Industrial output last month rose 0.9% from a year earlier – the lowest growth rate in a decade for September. Retail sales are plummeting, while consumer prices still are rising. Chinese and foreign economists now predict prolonged stagflation: low growth and high inflation. 'The economy is crashing hard,' says an Asian economist in Beijing. 'The slowdown is taking hold a lot more quickly and devastatingly than anyone had expected.'

The World Bank has defined Africa as passing through three stages, each roughly a decade long: modest growth following independence, a decade of stagnation, then a decade of decline.

...investment would have to fall by the equivalent of 4% of GNP in Japan, 3.75% in Britain, 2% in Germany and a more modest 1% in America. Declines of this size would turn the current downturn into deep depression. Deciding whether such a collapse is likely is difficult without understanding the reasons for the 1980s investment boom.

These largely irreversible mistakes have contributed greatly to an economic meltdown on a scale not witnessed in Europe since the Great Depression. Comparisons with the early 1930s reveal some frightening parallels.

16 Depressing metaphors. The numbered extracts talk about recession in metaphorical terms. Relate the metaphorical areas a–h to the extracts and underline the metaphorical expressions. (One extract contains two metaphors.)

a fire
b earthquakes
c sad music
d soft ground
e very calm winds
f excessive temperatures
g driving a car
h soap or similar substance

1 BRITAIN SINGS THE BLUES. Tony Balding, the managing director of Beaver Engineering, closed the door last weekend on the business his father founded in 1951.
2 With most of Europe in the doldrums, any sign of American economic strength will be welcomed by overseas companies seeking much-needed export markets.
3 A strong boom could quickly reignite inflation, forcing the Federal Reserve to slam on the brakes.
4 As the German economy has sunk into the recessionary mire, the Bundesbank has guided market rates down 1.5 per cent from their September 1992 peak.
5 As Japan's 'bubble' economy bursts, so thousands of companies are collapsing with it.
6 Freeing interest rates would send a sudden chill through an economy which, with inflation running at 11% and growth expected to reach 10% this year, looks set to overheat. However, the Korean economy still has formidable strengths.
7 Tony Millar, the chairman, said the group was not in a position to make a dividend forecast. The shares ended 25p down at 41p. The shock waves from Albert Fisher upset the other food distributors.

Green shoots and soft landings

bottom out
double-dip recession

trough

pick up
turn up

pick-up
turn-up
upturn
upswing

recover
recovery

strengthen

green shoots

During a recession people impatiently look for signs of a **recovery** or an **upturn**: signs that the economy is **recovering, strengthening, picking up**, or **turning up** and that things are getting better. Commentators then talk about a **pick-up, turn-up, upturn**, or **upswing** in the economy.

Or there may be a **double-dip recession**. The recession reaches its **trough** and **bottoms out**: the economy starts to improve, but then turns down again into a second trough.

In a recent British recession, one minister talked about seeing signs of recovery before anybody else could see them: he talked about **green shoots** and this expression is now used derisively in the context of unjustified optimism during recessions.

'The only recession-proof industry will be analysing the recession.'

There's considerable doubt the reports will clarify whether the economy is strengthening or weakening.

The recession is deepening rather than bottoming out, according to a survey of business expectations by Dun and Bradstreet.

New York's stock market has risen by 19% from its mid-January low thanks to hopes of economic recovery in America. Many economists reckon that America's recession, which began last summer, has now reached its trough; they predict that the economy will soon pick up.

For the past five quarters there has been a moderate recovery, but fears of a 'double dip' or 'triple dip' have remained because the upturn has been much weaker than in previous cycles.

Bond prices typically begin to rally about 12 months before the trough of the business cycle, just ahead of the peak in interest rates. Six months later (six months before the economic turn-up begins), equity prices start to take off.

Talbot insists he will wait for the economy to turn up and for trading conditions to improve before he sells, which means some time next year.

Things seemed brighter for a month or so. There seemed at last some sign of the elusive green shoots, with a bit of a pick-up in consumer spending.

'All the elements are in place to take advantage of an upswing in the market when it takes place – we don't know when that will be,' he said.

take off
soft landing

When a recession is over, and there is steady growth, the economy is said to **take off**.

Some commentators talk about the idea of a **soft landing**: moderate growth combined with low inflation, avoiding the usual excesses of booms.

◆ **LANGUAGE NOTE**

The noun corresponding to **take off** is **take-off**.

Although the American economy took off like a rocket after its early-1980s recession, Britain's economy was slower to pick up.

'The logical flaw in the whole concept of a soft landing is that there isn't any end,' says James Solloway, chief economist at Argus Research in New York. 'You either get more softness, ending up in a recession, or you take off again. You can't keep soft landing forever.'

17 **Perverse but true.** Read this leading article from the *Guardian*, written as Britain was coming out of a recent recession, and answer the questions.

AVOIDING A CHAIN REACTION

There is one overriding priority for the government between now and Budget day. It is to devise a scheme to prevent another totally unnecessary chain reaction of bankruptcies among small companies. Last year saw a record number of company collapses. They were, at least in part, a result of failure; the failure of companies to adjust to an unexpectedly steep recession and the failure of their banks, themselves fighting for survival, to keep them on a life support system until better times prevailed. This year's bankruptcies will be the result of problems of coping with success as the economy at long last moves haltingly towards recovery.

1 If a priority is overriding, is it important?

2 If you devise a scheme, you d _ _ _ _ _ n one.

3 In a chain reaction, A affects B, B affects C, C affects _, and so on.

4 Do steep recessions happen quickly?

bankruptcy 141 ⇑

5 If a person moves haltingly, do they halt?

It is a well-known, if perverse, fact of an economic upswing that it often accelerates the number of company collapses. Companies eagerly accept orders for which they won't be paid until completion many months later. Their working capital inevitably rises as they buy more components, expand stocks and put more workers on overtime. They turn to the banks expecting sympathy since they have orders in hand as potential collateral. But the banks, accustomed to taking a crude accounting stance instead of a long-term business view, see only big debts and a chance to pull the plug on companies at a time when their asset values are rising.

If all this happens during the recovery from a 'normal' recession, then it will happen frequently this time because the banks themselves have bombed-out balance sheets and will be even more reluctant to risk shareholders' money on what they see as risky rescues. ....

6 If something is perverse, is it logical and reasonable?

7 If X accelerates Y, does it slow it down?

working capital *126* ⇑

component *71* ⇑

stocks *74* ⇑

8 A stance on something is an o _ _ _ _ _ n.

9 If someone pulls the plug on someone or something, do they allow them to continue?

10 If you are reluctant to do something, you are h _ _ _ _ _ _ _ t to do it.

balance sheet *134* ⇑

The feelgood factor

feelgood factor

Commentators talk about the **feelgood factor** when discussing how prosperous and optimistic, or not, ordinary people feel, especially at a time of economic recovery. However, recent recoveries seem not to result automatically in people feeling good.

◆ **LANGUAGE NOTE**

Feelgood is also spelled with a hyphen and as two words.

'He's not the feel-good factor he used to be.'

The number of transactions in the housing market is rising strongly and this should be reflected in better numbers from the building societies. Despite the improving indicators, the 'feel good' factor, which comes with an upturn, is still missing. Unless governments can find ways of generating new jobs quickly, the UK will have to become used to unemployment levels close to three million.

18 **Feelgood without a job?** Read this extract from a book called *Jobshift* by William Bridges and answer the questions.

THE DEATH OF THE JOB

... Every day brings another story of 'job losses'. We are told the recession is over, but the proportion of the workforce that is 'jobless' has not fallen as it has after previous recessions. The government is trying to 'create jobs' by easing taxes and regulations, but says it should intervene more. We hear that the only way to protect jobs is to increase productivity, yet the result seems to be to make the jobs redundant.

When I was growing up, we used to read that by the year 2000 everyone would have to work only 30 hours a week and that the rest would be leisure time. But as we approach the year 2000, it seems more likely that half of us will work 60 hours a week and the rest of us will be unemployed. What is going wrong?

The reality is that what is disappearing today is not just a certain number of jobs, of jobs in certain industries or in one country – or even jobs in the developed world as a whole. What is disappearing is the very thing itself: the job.

The job is a social artefact, though it is so deeply embedded in our consciousness that most of us have forgotten its

1 If you intervene in something, you don't l _ _ _ _ e it a _ _ _ _ e.

2 If a government eases taxes, does it raise them?

3 If something is redundant, is it necessary?

4 The developed world is the i n d _ _ _ _ _ _ _ _ i z e d world.

5 If something is embedded in your consciousness, do you actively think about it?

artificiality, or the fact most societies since the beginning of time have done fine without jobs. In the pre-industrial past, people worked very hard, but they did not have jobs to frame and contain their activities. Then jobs became not only common but important: they were nothing less than the only widely-available path to security and success. Now they are disappearing. ...

6 Jobs were 'nothing less than' the only available path to security? Does this mean that they were the only path to security, or that there were other paths to security?

So what do people do without jobs? Some possibilities are obvious. you can start a business on your own; you can become an artist; you can become a consultant; you can do freelance work, or part-time work, or piecework in your own home. Under the pressure of dejobbing in organisations, more people than ever before are doing all of these things. But there is another answer. You can do what more and more people are doing: working within organisations, but under arrangements too fluid and idiosyncratic to be called jobs.

7 What word is used in this paragraph to talk about jobs disappearing?

8 If something is idiosyncratic, is it normal?

9 Fluid arrangements are not r i _ _ d.

'You won't last at Microsoft if your job is just a job.' That is how Teresa Stowell, a software design engineer, describes what it is like to work at the Seattle software powerhouse. To begin with people work any time and all the time, with no one keeping track of their hours, but with everyone watching their output. They are accountable not to conventional managers but to the project teams of which they are a part. ...

10 Do people clock on and off at Microsoft?

When a project ends, Microsoft employees move on to a new one, taking with them the reputation they earned on the last project. There are no standard career routes. 'If people want to change functions or they want to get different experiences, that's not frowned on at all. ... Employees drive their own development, and we need to design all

11 If you frown on something, you d i s _ _ _ _ _ _ _ _ of it.

of our management and our training programmes to support, augment and facilitate that development.' ...

Just as workers will need to be ready to shift from project to project within the same organisation, they should expect that much more frequently than in the past they will have to move from one organisation to another. Long-term employment is, for most workers, a thing of the past. The organisation will try to minimise these shifts, recognising that they are difficult and disruptive to the effectiveness of both the organisation and the worker. But both parties will have to make their long-term plans with the likelihood of such shifts in mind. ... Unless we begin soon to re-educate our workforces in these new expectations and the economic realities that have shaped them, we are in for decades of economic chaos that will damage our organisations and devastate several generations of workers. ...

12 Augment means i n _ _ _ _ _ _ .

13 Should workers be prepared to change projects?

14 If something is disruptive, is it easy to keep going as you were before?

15 If X shapes Y, does X have a lot of influence over the way Y develops?

16 Is devastation
a) slight damage, or
b) serious damage?

Crossword

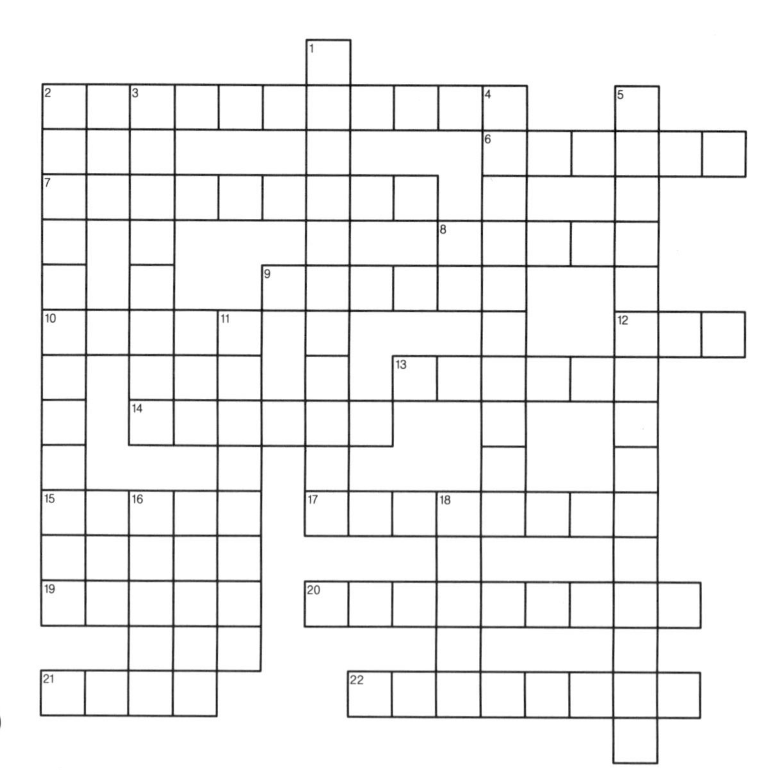

Across

2 Oil, precious metals, and cereals are examples of these (11)
6 Goods made for sale abroad are for ________ (6)
7 Key economic information that is often eagerly awaited (9)
8 Big increase; also a verb (5)
9 Prices don't just edge, they edge ________ (6)
10 This gives its owner an interest in the profits of the company (5)
12 Difference between value of imports and exports: trade ________ (3)
13 Good news on shares and growth, not so good on inflation and unemployment (6)
14 Share capital (6)
15 Low share turnover means ________ trading (5)
17 D as in GDP (8)
19 When shares do this, they fall; also a noun (5)
20 When shares do this, they increase greatly in value (4,5)
21 Increase, noun and verb (4)
22 Plural 13s (8)

Down

1 Profits not put into reserves are ________ to shareholders (11)
2 Barriers on the Hong Kong stock exchange? (7,5)
3 Trading of shares is like this most of the time (8)
4 Shares and bonds (10)
5 Currency dealing (7,8)
11 Shares as an investment medium (8)
16 Advances (5)
18 What an investment returns is what it ________ (5)

Answer key

1 What business are you in?

1 Business partners

1 business interests
2 business empire
3 business ventures
4 business school
5 business community
6 business leaders
7 business confidence

2 Corporate partners

1 corporate image
2 corporate ladder
3 corporate performance
4 corporate culture
5 corporate governance
6 corporate strategy
7 corporate collapses
8 corporate logo

a collapses
b culture
c strategies
d ladder
e governance
f performance
g logo, image

3 Wearing the corporate identity

1 No;
2 perhaps;
3 logo;
4 No;
5 Yes;
6 No;
7 well do you?

4 Key sector exercise

manufacturing

5 Unpopular privatizations

1a, 2b, 3a, 4d, 5a, 6c, 7a, 8b, 9a

6 Risky stakes?

1 Yes; 2 Yes; 3 No; 4 success; 5 No;
6 Yes; 7 power, influence; 8 b

7 Fingers in many pies

subsidiaries

8 Bid types

If a bid is	abortive contested derisory inadequate sweetened unsolicited unwelcome	it is	unsuccessful fought against insultingly low not enough improved unsought unwanted

9 Swallowing the poison pill

a, d, b, c, e, f

10 Giants and midgets

1a, 2e, 3c, 4c, 5c,. 6a, 7f, 8a, 9d,
10b, 11a

11 Company relationships 1

1 woo, woo;
2 courtship;
3 on-off;
4 leap into bed;
5 dowry;
6 ends in tears

12 Company relationships 2

1b, 2a, 3d, 4e, 5c

DANGEROUS LIAISONS

b AMD, in its trumpeting of this week's agreement with Fujitsu, seemed to take little account of the Japanese company's extensive network of relationships with western companies, including ICL, Siemens and Amdahl. Does it understand how it features, and could be manipulated, in Fujitsu's global battle against IBM?

a Equally, does IBM really understand where it figures in Toshiba's strategy of alliances with all and sundry? The same applies within the US itself, to IBM's place in Apple's growing spider's web of relationships - and vice versa.

c Alliances may give companies unprecedented flexibility. But, by the same token, they render them unstable. To revert to analogies from personal life, it is far easier to control one's destiny if one has just a couple of mutually compliant lovers than if one tries to run a series of ever-changing one-night stands.

13 Unwilling partners

Renault, Volvo in 'preliminary' talks: merger would create No. 4 auto firm.
a, c, d

Firmly embarked on new strategy – profile: Volvo.
b, e, f

14 Sticking to your knitting

1 excess;
2 Yes;
3 No;
4 No: 'abortive bid', 'Midland rejected the idea';
5 Yes;
6 No;
7 'sector' is used here meaning 'industry', rather than in contexts such as 'manufacturing sector' or 'public sector';
8 No;
9 No;
10 recession;
11 It concentrates on the things it is good at;
12 No;
13 Saatchi's attempt to buy Midland Bank;
14 mistake

15 MBO story

a, d, b, c, e

Crossword solution

	C	O	N	G	L	O	M	E	R	A	T	E	
	O						U			S			
	M	E	R	G	E		L			S	P	I	N
	P					S	T	A	K	E			
W	A	R	D				I			T		A	
	N			G	I	A	N	T		S	E	L	L
	Y			R			A					L	
		P	R	E	D	A	T	O	R		B	I	D
				E			I			P		A	
O		C	O	N	T	R	O	L		A		N	
F		O					N			R		C	
F	I	R	M	S			A			E		E	
		E			H	O	L	D	I	N	G	S	
										T			

2 People and organizations

1 Types of business people

1 prominent, leading,
2 powerful,
3 successful,
4 local,
5 foreign,
6 small

a foreign,
b small,
c successful,
d local,
e prominent,
f leading,
g powerful

2 Entrepreneurial combinations

1b, 2a, 3g, 4f, 5e, 6d, 7c

3 Executive exercise

toy
(plural in the last two extracts)

4 Role-playing

The person who chairs board meetings is the chairman or chairwoman. The position is often combined with that of managing director, who may be responsible for the day-to-day running of the company. This responsibility is made specific in the titles chief executive, chief executive officer, or CEO.

Some companies also have a chief operating officer in addition to or instead of a CEO.

5 The Good Board Guide

1 health, comfort, and prosperity;
2 wealth;
3 b;
4 Because books about business are not famous for their elegant writing;
5 F Scott Fitzgerald, American novelist, and Queen Christina of Sweden are not usually quoted in books like this whereas Machiavelli, famous for Machiavellian methods, and Peters and Waterman, authors of the successful 1980s business book *In Search of Excellence*, are;
6 Yes;
7 relationship;
8 atmosphere;
9 Yes;
10 No

6 Ruthless tactics?

1 Animals, by people hunting on other people's land without permission;
2 No, disapproval;
3 No;
4 No;
5 No

7 Model execs?

1 No; 2b; 3 No; 4 No; 5 No; 6 rich; 7 excessive; 8 Yes; 9 worry; 10 Yes, in the first of the two senses

8 Failure-related pay

1 booted,
2 fortune,
3 package,
4 compensation,
5 pay-off,
6 goodbyes,
7 executive

9 Rocket fuel for banks

a, c, d, e, b

10 Labour exercise

1 labour mobility
2 labor unions (in Britain, trade unions)
3 skilled labour
4 labour shortage
5 manual labour
6 cheap labour
7 labour disputes
8 labour relations

11 Personnel criticism

1 Yes; 2 cowboy; 3 Yes;
4 employers, employees, management, labour;
5 making; 6a; 7 No

12 Personnel problems

The article is written in American English because:

1) it mentions 'hires' as a noun meaning people who have been hired,
2) it uses 'quit' where a writer of British English would talk about people who 'leave' a company, and
3) it uses 'terminate', where, again, a writer of British English would talk about people who 'leave' a company.

13 Corporate weight reduction

a diet;
b health farm;
c corpulence;
d slimming;
e fatter

14 Radical empowerment

1 No; 2 No; 3 decide; 4 Yes; 5 Yes; 6 bust; 7 No; 8 survive; 9 odd; 10 No; 11 Yes

15 Parade of euphemisms

let go, terminate, discharge, fire, sack, axe, give someone the boot, push, chop, release

The following expressions do not exactly mean 'dismiss', but might be used in a situation where a company is getting rid of people:

People 'retire' (even if they are being forced to leave), they leave by mutual consent, they part company to spend more time with their family, they exit the organization, they are given the opportunity to look elsewhere, they pursue an alternative career, or they accept a fresh challenge.

Their careers plateau.

They are told that there is a process of involuntary separation, downsizing, rightsizing, rationalization, decruitment, deselection, displacement, retrenchment, or re-engineering.

They may be told: 'You are surplus to requirements', 'Your future lies elsewhere', 'We can't make the best use of your talents'.

16 Finding the right job

1 a)
The article discusses the efforts of Lord Strathalmond, a peer, to find work. These efforts might be described as 'peer pressure', so using the phrase in an unusual way;
2 off-the-peg;
3 No;
4 they ask people who went to their school if those people have a job for them;
5 No: 'uphearted' does not exist;
6 compulsory;
7 b;
8 No;
9 No

17 The survivors of downsizing

1 load;
2 No;
3 Yes;
4 close;
5 change;
6 secretary;
7 No;
8 repeated, copied;
9 No;
10 let, go;
11 overworked

Crossword solution

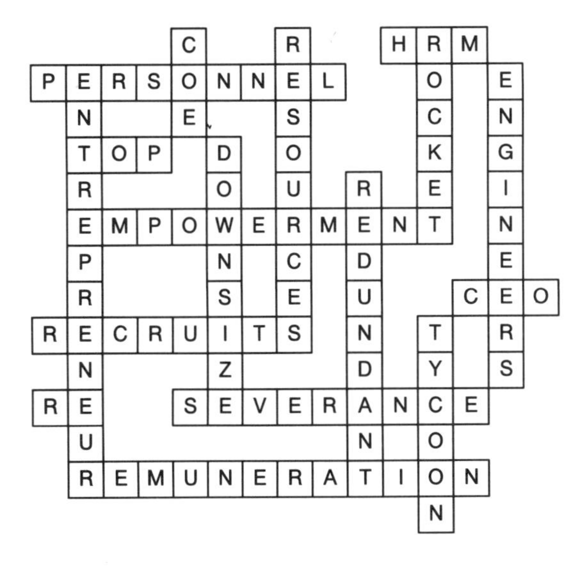

3 Research, development, and production

1 Welcome innovations?

television, air conditioner, dishwasher, microwave oven, video-cassette recorder, automatic coffee maker, remote control, computer, fax machine, telephone answering machine, compact disk player, Walkman

2 What's in a name?

1c, 2d, 3f, 4a, 5b, 6e

3 Taking on a giant

a, b, e, d, c, f

4 Small is beautiful

a, c, e, d, b, f

5 Drawn to the Sunbelt

1 Utilities are things like electricity and water. Benefits are things in addition to basic pay, such as sick pay, pension rights and so on;
2 No;
3 subcontracts;
4 Yes;
5 a;
6 consider

6 Production partners

1 production facilities
2 production process
3 production line
4 production cycle
5 production budget
6 production target
7 production cuts

7 Undisciplined robots

1 No; 2 Yes; 3 bet; 4 No; 5 Yes; 6 Yes

8 Lost in translation

Missing words:
1d, 2b, 3a, 4d, 5a, 6a, 7a, 8b, 9f, 10a, 11c, 12a, 13b, 14e, 15a, 16b, 17c

Answers to questions:
1 Yes; 2 horses; 3 Yes; 4 No: it means that Japanese methods never seem to work as well when they are 'translated', are brought in, by western companies; 5 competitive; 6 Yes; 7 No; 8 a; 9 No; 10 No

9 Philosophy quiz

1a, 2d, 3c, 4b

10 Fad backlash

1 No; 2 No; 3 No; 4 improvement; 5 Yes; 6 No; 7 agree; 8 rid; 9 b

Crossword solution

	S							L	E	A	D	I	N	G	
O	U	T	S	O	U	R	C	E		S		N			
	B							A		S		V			
			I	N	F	R	I	N	G	E	M	E	N	T	
	S		N				N			M		N		E	
R	U	S	T	B	E	L	T			B		T		C	
	P		E				E			L		O		H	
	P		R	E	E	N	G	I	N	E	E	R	I	N	G
	L		M				R			D		I		O	
H	I	T	E	C	H		A					E		L	
	E		D			S	T	A	T	E		S		O	
	R		I				I		I					G	
		B	A	C	K	R	O	O	M	B	O	Y		I	
			T				N		E					E	
L	I	C	E	N	S	E					H	O	U	S	E

4 Products, markets, and marketing

1 Consumer combinations

1 consumer durables
2 consumer boom
3 consumer boycott
4 consumer confidence
5 consumer protection
6 consumer behaviour
7 consumer backlash

2 Competitive expressions

formidable, fierce, cut-throat, stiff, tough, significant, intense

3 Market partners

A market economy is one where things are bought and sold freely and not under government control. In a market economy, prices are decided by market forces, the factors that influence the demand for things, their availability, and consequently their price. Market price is used to indicate that a price has been 'decided' by the market, and not in some other way, for example by the government. Market place means the same as market. Market research is the gathering of information on markets, products and consumers: on what people need, want, and buy; how and when they buy; and why they buy one thing rather than another.

4 Abbreviated segments

1 Double Income, No Kids
2 First-time Expectant Mothers
3 Downwardly-Mobile Professionals
4 Green Upwardly-Mobile Professionals
5 Burnt-Out But Opulent
6 Single Women Earning Lots in London

5 Goods as services, and vice-versa

MANUFACTURING MYTHS

Dividing their labour and specialising, people buy goods and services from each other. Car workers eat hamburgers: hamburger flippers watch films; film producers buy cars. All depend on each other, for each provides the others with something they want.

None is the place where the buck starts, or stops. But their jobs are not equal. Some activities earn more than others, broadly because they add more value, create more wealth.

Once, it was true that the most value was added in manufacturing. No longer. Some factories add lots of value, some little. Lots of value is added in services. Nor is there a relevant distinction between manufacturing and services, but it has become much harder to distinguish it.

Any product: a car, a semi-conductor, a shirt, is a bundle of different processes, some of them services, some of them manufacturing. The way that bundle is tied together has changed.

The designer of the Morris Minor and the Mini, Alec Issigonis, provided a service. Yet statistically he was a manufacturer, since he was employed as a car maker. In the 1950s and 1960s firms tended to perform many of their own services. What if Issigonis had gone off to run his own car design and engineering firm? At a stroke, the proportion of Britain's GDP in manufacturing would have fallen and that in services would have risen.

That trend, of contracting services out rather than performing them in-house, was common everywhere in the 1980s. It is one big reason why manufacturing's share fell. ...

6 Innovative nightmares

1b, 2a, 3e, 4d, 5c, 6c

7 Product combinations

1 product mix, range, line, portfolio
2 product lifecycle
3 product positioning
4 product placement

1d, 2e, 3b, 4c, 5a, 6g, 7f

8 Loss leader package holidays

a, d, b, c, e

9 Brand dilution

1 break; 2 Yes; 3 No; 4 Yes; 5 candy; 6 soap powder and a sticky chocolate bar respectively; 7 No; 8 cigarettes; 9 Because it's normally associated with chocolate and the two products are incompatible; 10 b; 11 No. 'In the pipeline' is used to talk about things in general that are in preparation or about to arrive; 12 Yes

10 Price logic

low-priced

11 One country's export is another's dumping

a, e, g, c, d, b, f, h

12 Market logic

matched extracts: 1e, 2a, 3d, 4b, 5c
missing word: mass-market

13 Competing with yourself?

1g, 2b, 3e, 4f, 5a, 6d, 7c, 8f, 9f, 10h

14 Lite lies?

a, c, b, d, e, f

15 Forms of selling

1b, 2a, 3f, 4c, 5d, 6e

16 The end of shopping as we know it?

a, f, e, b, d, c

17 The end of TV advertising as we know it?

1a, 2b, 3a, 4c, 5b, 6f, 7b, 8b, 9a, 10e, 11f, 12d, 13e, 14e, 15a

18 Promotions from hell

1, b, iii; 2, e, ii; 3, d, iv; 4, c, i; 5, a, v

19 Is less more?

1 No;
2 a;
3 change, attitude;
4 More quantity: customers used to think that more quantity of a product was a good thing, now they don't;
5 Yes;
6 throw, away;
7 Yes;
8 Yes

20 The end of marketing as we know it?

1 kill off, abolish;
2 concentrate;
3 Yes;
4 No;
5 a;
6 No;
7 Yes;
8 handicap

Crossword solution

	C	O	M	P	E	T	I	T	I	V	E			
	A		E							O			G	
	N		R		L		M	A	I	L	S	H	O	T
	N	I	C	H	E			D		U			O	
	I		H		A			V		M			D	
	B	R	A	N	D	A	W	A	R	E	N	E	S	S
	A		N		E			N						E
	L		D	I	R	E	C	T		P		P		G
	I		I					A		A		L		M
	Z		S		J			G		C		A		E
R	E	V	E	N	U	E		E		K	E	Y		N
	D				N					A		E		T
		M	A	R	K	E	T	I	N	G		R		
										E		S		

5 The bottom line

1 Sales logic

target: singular in the first three lines, plural in the others

2 Cost-cutting exercise

severe		measure
drastic		programme
stringent	**cost-cutting**	exercise
huge		campaign
aggressive		scheme

3 Spend function

1. 15,000 to 20,000 companies have five or more locations. Together, these companies spend an estimated $12 billion annually on telecommunications services. (Verb)
2. Advertisers spend $2 billion a year in the production of commercials. (Verb)
3. It takes great courage to maintain a high marketing spend in a downturn. (Noun)
4. Not for nothing do drug companies spend more than £1 million on medical journal advertising. (Verb)
5. Radio takes only 2% of Britain's total advertising spend. (Noun)
6. Some companies spend months carrying out market research before launching a magazine. (Verb)
7. The necessary increase in marketing spend may mean profits slip a little in the second half. (Noun)

4 Diseconomies of scale

1	bleak, rosy;	5	machine;
2	more similar;	6	dominate;
3	expert;	7	No;
4	Yes;	8	No

5 Cost, sales, and profit logic

1a, 2a, 3e, 4b, 5d, 6f, 7c

6 Margin for error?

1e, 2d, 3a, 4b, 5c

7 Cash flow logic

1h, 2g, 3a, 4d, 5e, 6a, 7c

8 Overdraft alternatives

Around 85 per cent of UK exports are still financed by the traditional bank overdraft, despite the advantages of using factoring companies – which buy debts in return for an immediate cash payment, take over debtor records and provide a collection service for clients.

Overdrafts, indeed, are seldom used effectively to finance overseas trade. Most banks seek security for loans, often using a company's assets including its trade debts to support any overdraft. They will usually lend up to 60 per cent of the value of a current UK receivable, but they still will not lend anything against the value of foreign trade debts.

9 Partners in debt

1a, f; 2e; 3c; 4b; 5d

i The aircraft leasing company owes $5.5 billion, and is deeply embroiled in debt-restructuring talks with shareholders, bankers and aircraft manufacturers.

ii But the biggest danger of all lies in the huge corporate debt burden. A prolonged period of falling prices raises the real level of that debt, and makes it harder for companies to service it. It is a sobering thought on the golf courses around Tokyo. Many of the courses were built in the boom years of the late 1980s, on the back of huge borrowings. Falling green fees may be good news for golfers, but the courses need more revenue, not less, to meet their debt-servicing costs.

iii Stronger demand will lift Forte's profits, while lower interest rates will cut the cost of its debt repayments.

iv Though there is pressure across the British banking industry to take a tough line on loans, bankers will reschedule debts if they can see some hope.

v Ten years ago, Mexico's announcement that it could not service its debt launched the 1980s debt crisis. Today, Mexico's public debt burden, successfully renegotiated, is a smaller proportion of the country's wealth than that of most industrialized countries.

10 Can brands be valued as intangible assets?

a, f, c, b, d, e, g

11 Leverage logic

1c, 2f, 3e, 4a, 5a, 6d, 7d, 8b, 9b, 10b, 11c, 12a, 13a

12 Furious window dressing

1 exaggerate;
2 No;
3 dishonest;
4 No;
5 investors;
6 No;
7 No;
8 the real financial situation of the company

13 Flowing through to the bottom line

1c, 2d, 3e, 4g, 5f, 6a, 7b

14 Troubleshooting specialist

1 No; 2 Yes; 3 Yes; 4 Yes; 5 Yes; 6 Well, would you? 7 deteriorates; 8 Yes; 9 b; 10 No

15 Humble record breaker

1 hopes, ambitions;
2 range;
3 Yes;
4 No;
5 No;
6 No: trappings are outward signs, for example of wealth;
7 No

16 Success in failure?

a corpse, undertaker;
b sweep up the debris, salvage the wreckage;
c spoils;
d pull the rug;
e recession;
f cash-strapped

Crossword solution

	S												A
D	E	B	T	S			C						S
	L				S		R		R				S
	F		C	E	A	S	E		E		B		E
	F		A		L		A	C	C	O	U	N	T
B	I	L	L		V		T		E		S		
	N		L	I	A	B	I	L	I	T	I	E	S
B	A	D			G		V		V		N		
	N			L	E	V	E	R	A	G	E	D	
	C			O		A			B		S		
	I			A		R			L	O	S	S	
I	N	T	A	N	G	I	B	L	E			T	
	G					A			S	H	O	R	T
		P	A	Y	A	B	L	E				E	
						L						A	
			S	A	L	E	S	V	O	L	U	M	E

6 Towards the feelgood factor

1 Bourses of the world

a, c, d, e, b, f

2 Does it matter where you are?

1 No;
2 well-dressed, well-off;
3 No;
4 Yes;
5 secure;
6 take;
7 competitors;
8 Because London is open when markets in Japan and America are closed;
9 b;
10 No;
11 Because they feel they want to be face to face with them when being advised on something so crucial.

3 Market players

1c, 2a, 3f, 4b, 5g, 6d, 7e

4 Cash call crisis

1 excessive;
2 investors;
3 Yes;
4 No;
5 painful;
6 No;
7 No

5 Critics of derivatives

1 reaction;
2 investment;
3 No;
4 Yes;
5 Yes;
6 c;
7 Yes

6 Dull or frenzied or something else?

The actual word used is in brackets.
1c (hectic), 2a (light), 3d (frenetic), 4d (frenzied), 5d (frenetic), 6b (mixed), 7a (dull), 8a (weak), 9b (erratic), 10b (mixed)

7 Market logic

1 recover,
2 recovered,
3 recovers,
4 recovered,
5 recovered,
6 recovering,
7 recovery

8 Wrongdoing 1

1c, 2h, 3b, 4g, 5a, 6f, 7d, 8e

9 Wrongdoing 2

1b, 2e, 3a, 4c, 5d, 6f

10 Piles of cash

Earnings not distributed are reserves, which may be used to finance a company's development in capital spending in investment, or paid out in a later period to shareholders. A company with a lot of reserves is said to have, or sit on, a cash pile or cash mountain. Like share capital or equity, reserves are part of shareholders' funds.

11 Rising and falling prices: verbs

1 climbed,
2 tumbled,
3 shot ahead,
4 leapt,
5 edged up,
6 slid,
7 skyrocketed,
8 plummeted,
9 slumped,
10 crumbled

12 Rising and falling prices: nouns

1 decline,
2 hike,
3 dip,
4 nose-dive,
5 collapse,
6 slip,
7 leap,
8 slump,
9 surge,
10 collapse

13 Massacre and meltdown

1d; 2f, a; 3c; 4b; 5h; 6g; 7e

14 Diamonds are not forever

1 diamonds;
2 healthy;
3 point;
4 criterion;
5 Yes;
6 smaller;
7 Yes;
8 bigger;
9 left

15 Weakening nouns

1f, 2b, 3g, 4a, 5c, 6e, 7d

16 Depressing metaphors

1c; 2e; 3a, g; 4d; 5h; 6f; 7b

17 Perverse but true

1 Yes;
2 design;
3 D;
4 Yes;
5 No;
6 No;
7 No;
8 opinion;
9 No;
10 hesitant

18 Feelgood without a job?

1 leave, alone;
2 No;
3 No;
4 industrialized;
5 No;
6 they were the only path;
7 dejobbing;
8 No;
9 rigid;
10 No;
11 disapprove;
12 increase;
13 Yes;
14 No;
15 Yes;
16 b

Crossword solution

						D									
C	O	M	M	O	D	I	T	I	E	S			F		
H		O				S				E	X	P	O	R	T
I	N	D	I	C	A	T	O	R		C			R		
N		E				R			S	U	R	G	E		
E		R			H	I	G	H	E	R			I		
S	H	A	R	E		B				I			G	A	P
E		T		Q		U		U	P	T	U	R	N		
W		E	Q	U	I	T	Y			I			E		
A				I		E				E			X		
L	I	G	H	T		D	O	M	E	S	T	I	C		
L		A		I					A				H		
S	L	I	D	E		R	O	A	R	A	H	E	A	D	
		N		S					N				N		
R	I	S	E				U	P	S	W	I	N	G	S	
													E		

Index

Acknowledgements

The author and publisher are grateful to the following for permission to reproduce the extracts and cartoons on the pages indicated:

Extracts:

Page 4, 'Corporate Identity: The Executive Uniform' Nicole Twosin, *Independent on Sunday;*
Page 8, 'Disgusted' © *The Economist,* 11.3.95;
Page 10, 'Biotech goes Glitzy' © *The Economist,* 30.8.92;
Page 14, 'Time Warner in Anti-takeover Move' *Financial Times,* 21.1.94;
Page 17, 'Lines across the Water' © *The Economist,* 5.6.93;
Page 18, 'Dangerous Liaisons' *Financial Times;*
Page 19, 'Renault, Volvo in "Preliminary" Talks' Reprinted by permission of *The Wall Street Journal* © 1989 Dow Jones & Company, Inc. All Rights Reserved Worldwide;
Page 19, 'Firmly Embarked on New Strategy' *Financial Times,* 19.12.94;
Page 22, 'After the Party, it's Back to Basics' *Financial Times,* 16.8.94;
Page 24, 'The Most Important Deal of Your Life' *Financial Times,* 1.12.94;
Page 32, 'The Corporate Board' Reprinted from the August 1992 edition, with permission from *Director Publications;*
Page 35, 'Poacher Turned TV Star' *Financial Times,* 17.1.94;
Page 37, 'Wealth Eludes the Salaryman' *Financial Times,* 31.1.94;
Page 40, 'A Racket in Need of Reform' © *The Economist,* 27.8.94;
Page 42, 'Rocket Scientists with a Billion-Dollar Brain' *Financial Times,* 21.5.94;
Page 45, 'HRM: Big Hat but no Cattle?' Sue Fernie and David Metcalf, *Financial Times,* 6.4.94;
Page 49, 'When Slimming is not Enough' © *The Economist,* 3.9.94;
Page 50, 'Management Lessons from Brazil' © *The Economist,* 26.3.93;
Page 53, 'Softening the Blow 1' *Financial Times,* 29.4.94;
Page 53, 'Softening the Blow 2' *Financial Times,* 4.7.94;
Page 54, 'Peer Pressure for Jobs' *Financial Times,* 8.6.94;
Page 56, 'Overwork: the Nineties Disease' Annabel Ferriman, *Independent on Sunday;*
Page 60, 'Little Wishes from the Big Dream' Reprinted by permission of *The Wall Street Journal* © 1989 Dow Jones & Company, Inc. All Rights Reserved Worldwide;
Page 61, 'Who Steals my Name' © *The Economist,* 26.3.94;
Page 62, 'Judgement is Music to Sony's Ears' Natasha Narayan and Ian Katz, *The Guardian;*
Page 64, 'Mastering the Machine' *The Economist,* 19.10.91;
Page 66, 'Lone Eagles Nest in the Rockies' *Financial Times,* 23.5.94;
Page 70, 'When GM's Robots Run Amok' © *The Economist,* 31.8.91;
Page 72, 'Manufacturing and the Price of Outsourcing' © *The Economist,* 31.8.91;
Page 74, 'Philosophy Quiz' Peter Grimsdale, *Independent on Sunday,* 11.11.90;
Page 75, 'Philosophy Quiz' Simon Caulkin, *The Guardian;*
Page 75, 'Philosophy Quiz' *Financial Times,* 4.1.94 and 1.8.94;
Page 76, 'Take a Clean Sheet of Paper' © *The Economist,* 1.5.93;
Page 86, 'Manufacturing Myths' © *The Economist,* 9.11.91;
Page 87, 'Wakey Wakey' *Financial Times,* 8.8.94;
Page 90, 'Travel Agents Warned over Adverts' Harvey Elliott, *The Times,* 1.8.92 © Times Newspapers Limited, 1992;
Page 92, 'Stretching a Brand to the Break Point' Helen Jones, *Independent on Sunday;*
Page 96, 'EU Steel Dumping Claim' *Financial Times,* 2.8.94;
Page 99, 'Cannibalising Up or Down?' © *The Economist,* 15.8.92;
Page 103, 'The Interactive Bazaar Opens' © *The Economist,* 20.8.94;
Page 105, 'Heinz Drops TV Adverts' *Financial Times,* 3.5.94;
Page 107, 'Promotions from Hell' Rhys Williams, *The Independent;*
Page 108, 'Business and the Environment' *Financial Times,* 7.12.94;
Page 111, 'Death of the Brand Manager' © *The Economist,* 9.4.94;
Page 118, 'The Fall of Big Business' © *The Economist,* 17.4.93;
Page 121, 'Why CDs are Music to the Ears at Polygram' Ben Laurance, *The Guardian;*
Page 123, 'Hey Presto for Business' Jane Bird, *The Times,* 18.9.92;
Page 125, 'Controlling the Cash Flow' *Financial Times,* 19.2.94;
Page 127, 'Factoring's Unsung Role for Exporters' Mark Runiewicz, *Financial Times,* 17.5.94;
Page 131, 'IBM Plunges to Bottom of Brand Name Value League' *Financial Times,* 11.7.94;
Page 136, 'Revealed' John Cassidy et al, *Sunday Times,* 16.8.92, © Times Newspapers Limited, 1992;

Page 139, 'The Flamboyant Troubleshooter' *Financial Times*, 12.9.94;
Page 141, 'The Humbling of Bankrupt Kevin Maxwell' Richard Ford and Geoff King, *The Times*, 4.9.94, © Times Newspapers Limited, 1994;
Page 145, 'Going Bust Means Boom Time' *Today*, 2.6.92, © News (UK) Ltd;
Page 147, 'Touring the Bourses' © *The Economist*, 4.7.92;
Page 150, 'Why London?' © *The Economist*, 4.5.91;
Page 153, 'Millions Wiped Out' Jeff Randall, *The Times*, 13.9.92, © Times Newspapers Limited, 1992;
Page 155, 'A Distracting Sideshow' Reprinted by permission of *The Wall Street Journal*, © 1989 Dow Jones & Company, Inc. All Rights Reserved Worldwide;
Page 160, 'Loan Leak Rumour Sweeps Market' Neil Bennett, *The Times*, 5.9.92, © Times Newspapers Limited, 1992;
Page 175, 'An Economy's Best Friend' © *The Economist*, 16.11.91;
Page 181, 'Avoiding a Chain Reaction' *The Guardian*;
Page 183, 'The Death of the Job' from *Jobshift: How to Prosper in a Workplace Without Jobs*, Nicholas Brealey Publishing Ltd, London 1995.

Cartoons:
Page 2, © A.L.I. Press Agency Ltd;
Page 7 (top), originally published in *The Spectator*;
Page 7 (bottom), Peter Till;
Page 8, Chris Riddell, *The Economist*;
Page 9, © A.L.I. Press Agency Ltd;
Page 24, © A.L.I. Press Agency Ltd;
Page 29, reproduced by permission of *Punch*;
Page 30, © A.L.I. Press Agency Ltd;
Page 32, reproduced by permission of *Punch*;
Page 34, © A.L.I. Press Agency Ltd;
Page 36 (left), © A.L.I. Press Agency Ltd;
Page 36 (right), © A.L.I. Press Agency Ltd;
Page 39, Chris Riddell, *The Economist*;
Page 41 (top), Geoff Thompson, *The World's Greatest Business Cartoons*, Exley Publications Ltd;
Page 41 (bottom), © A.L.I. Press Agency Ltd;
Page 46 (left), reproduced by permission of *Punch*;
Page 46 (right), © A.L.I. Press Agency Ltd;
Page 47, reproduced by permission of *Punch*;
Page 48, Signe Wilkinson, USA, Cartoonists & Writers Syndicate;
Page 49, David Simonds, *The Economist*;
Page 52 (top left), © A.L.I. Press Agency;
Page 52 (top right), reproduced by permission of *Punch*;
Page 52 (bottom), reproduced by permission of *Punch*;
Page 55, © A.L.I. Press Agency Ltd;
Page 63 (left), © A.L.I. Press Agency Ltd;
Page 63 (right), © A.L.I. Press Agency Ltd;
Page 67, © A.L.I. Press Agency Ltd;
Page 80, © A.L.I. Press Agency Ltd;
Page 84, reproduced by permission of *Punch*;
Page 88, originally published in *The Spectator*;
Page 96, originally published in *The Spectator*;
Page 103, DOONESBURY © 1994 G.B. Trudeau. Reprinted with permission of Universal Press Syndicate. All rights reserved;
Page 111, Chris Priestley, *The Economist*;
Page 126, © A.L.I. Press Agency Ltd;
Page 134, reproduced by permission of *Punch*;
Page 135, reproduced by permission of *Punch*;
Page 148, © A.L.I. Press Agency Ltd;
Page 159, © A.L.I. Press Agency Ltd;
Page 160, © A.L.I. Press Agency Ltd;
Page 164, Martin Honeysett, *The World's Greatest Business Cartoons*, Exley Publications Ltd;
Page 174, © A.L.I. Press Agency Ltd;
Page 177 (top), © A.L.I. Press Agency Ltd;
Page 177 (bottom), Payne © 1995, United Feature Syndicate. Reprinted by permission;
Page 179, © 1993, Washington Post Writers Group. Reprinted with permission;
Page 180, reproduced by permission of *Punch*;
Page 182, © *The Independent*.

Every effort has been made to contact the owners of copyright material. The publishers apologize for any omissions and will be glad to rectify these when the title is reprinted.